DISC THE RISEN CHRIST

CARDINAL CARLO MARTINI ON LENT AND EASTER

Carlo M. Martini
TRANSLATED BY Demetrio S. Yocum

Paulist Press
New York / Mahwah, NJ

Interior image by Sogno Lucido / Shutterstock.com

Cover art by Andrea del Sarto (c. 1487–1530). *Last Supper*, center section. 1526–1527. Fresco, Refectory of the Convent. S. Michele a San Salvi. (Scala/Ministero per I Beni e le Attività culturali / Art Resource, NY)

Cover and book design by Lynn Else

Library of Congress Control Number: 2015946445

ISBN 978-0-8091-4943-8 (paperback)
ISBN 978-1-58768-534-7 (e-book)

Published by Paulist Press
997 Macarthur Boulevard
Mahwah, New Jersey 07430

www.paulistpress.com

Printed and bound in the
United States of America

Contents

Introduction   v

I. The Eucharist as the Foreshadowing of Easter   1
  1. The Cross Is the Door   1
  2. Jesus' Testament   7
  3. Eucharist as Gift of Life   9
  4. *You Also Should Do as I Have Done to You*   20
  5. Church Means to Serve   26
  6. He Loves Us unto the End   33

II. Christ Is Risen from the Dead   49
  1. A Historical Event That Changes History 49
  2. A Shout of Joy, a Cry of Victory   65
  3. The Christian Response to Death   83
  4. Called by Name   92
  5. We Do Not Understand, but We Will   97
  6. The Risen Christ Is with Us   111
  7. Living as Resurrected   126

III. Pentecost: The Fulfillment of the
  Easter Mystery   131
  1. The Spirit of Renewal   131
  2. The Celebration of the Birth of the Church   136
  3. Promise and Testimony   142

Introduction

The days of Holy Week are an invitation to read and reflect on the various liturgical texts in order to enter into the various aspects of the Easter mystery; better yet, to let this mystery enter into us, as this mystery is greater than us; it is not we who seek it, it is the mystery that comes to us. If we open the doors of our hearts, the mystery of God's Passover, Christ's passing over from this world to the Father, the mystery of his passion, the mystery of our own passage from death to life, will enter and fill us by the very power of the Holy Spirit and through the efficacious power of the sacraments of the Church.

These are the words that Archbishop of Milan, Cardinal Carlo Maria Martini, used to speak to his parishioners on the occasion of a Holy Thursday. In order to be filled with the mystery of the resurrection, letting it reach the very depths of our hearts, we must at least focus on it, possibly in an attentive manner, and put ourselves in the best frame of mind to welcome it. This book of reflections by Cardinal Martini on the celebration of the Easter season wants to be a simple tool to help us to open to the Easter event and a source of spiritual meditation to approach the sacraments—that other great and powerful means (after and with the Holy Spirit) for the Divine Mystery to enter into the life of Christians—in a less distracted manner and with more awareness.

To further emphasize that the mystery of Easter cannot be penetrated by an intellectual or exegetical effort on the part of the priest or the faithful whom he accompanies, but rather by a willingness to be malleable instruments in the hands of the Lord and to be led by the Spirit, we turn to the humble words of a *Confessio Laudis* (confession of praise) delivered by the cardinal during another homily. Recalling the page of the prophet Ezekiel in which a multitude of dry bones resume flesh and life through the breath of the Spirit, the then archbishop of Milan said,

> The Lord did the same thing in the early days of the Church with the scattered limbs of the

apostles, the first disciples; and, in a similar manner, the Lord has done with my own life, in particular through the gift of my priestly ordination: my poverty, my dry bones, were enlivened and transformed by the Spirit, which should be honored and glorified for all the good I have been able to accomplish thus far. It is the Holy Spirit that by its own power has acted and is acting in me, helping me to understand, to put into practice, Jesus' words, his deeds, his behavior. It is the Spirit that has guided me in the reading and interpretation of the Scriptures, as mentioned by Pope John Paul II in his letter where he says that, in all my pastoral activities, the first place has always been occupied by the Scriptures, as it should be for a pastor of souls.

Cardinal Martini's reflections proposed in this volume revolve primarily around three major themes: the Eucharist, the Easter of resurrection, and Pentecost.

In the institution of the Eucharist at the Last Supper, we can see the prefiguration of what happens in Christ's passion and resurrection (Jesus' free gift of life for a sinful humanity, for every sinner), and at the same time, Jesus' merciful legacy for his Church, the assurance of his own presence now and forever through the sacraments. Martini's meditations on this theme in the end become an invitation to a more vivid Christian experience around the table of the Eucharist, starting from a renewed spiritual commitment that culminates in a more generous practice of charity.

The Lord's resurrection on Easter Day is the central theme of the entire book, and it could not have been otherwise given that this event radically changes the existence of all humanity. The joy of Easter is an irresistible message that needs to be spread to every human being because it is a simple personal call that touches each one individually, as it was for Mary Magdalene, for whom it was enough to be called by name by the risen Christ to finally understand her joy and her own salvation.

The theme of the outpouring of the Holy Spirit at Pentecost as the birth of the early Church naturally becomes then an exhortation to bear witness to the risen Christ to all people. It is Cardinal Martini himself who in one of his vivid homilies recalled John Paul II's penetrating words on the birth of the early Church and, consequently, the spreading to the entire world of the Word of God: "*Wherever you are in the world, you are, with your vocation, 'for the universal Church,' through your mission 'in a given local Church.'*" Thus, the vocation for the universal Church is realized within the structure of the local church: "Every effort must be made," added the pope, "in order that 'consecrated life' may develop in the individual local Churches, in order that it may contribute to their spiritual building up, in order that it may constitute their particular strength."[1] The service and enrichment of the local Church brings about the service and enrichment of the universal Church, because the universal Church exists in a communion that does not tolerate the exclusion or limitation of the particular churches. Unity with the universal Church through the local church: this is the way.

Thus, even through the dissemination of his meditations on the liturgy and on the Word, the pastor of souls tries to help every Christian to pay attention to their personal call to salvation and to be open to the Holy Spirit.

---

1. Address of His Holiness John Paul II to the Superiors General of Men's Religious Orders, http://w2.vatican.va/content/john-paul-ii/en/speeches/1978/documents/hf_jp-ii_spe_19781124_superiori-generali.html (emphasis added).

The Eucharist as the Foreshadowing of Easter

1. THE CROSS IS THE DOOR

I would like to begin this series of reflections with a prayer: Lord Jesus, we as Christians wish to penetrate the mystery of your cross and ask you, especially during the Easter Triduum, to do so with the same love and contemplative power of St. Charles Borromeo, who in one of his homilies said, "Truly happy are those who have impressed in their hearts Christ crucified; oh, happy are those who, at every moment, are able to fix in their memories his passion that gives life. I dare say that, in some way, they would never be able to sin."

Therefore, we must ask for the gift of this assiduous memory and meditation of our Lord's passion, so that it can accompany us especially during Holy Week and help us to penetrate the heart of St. Charles Borromeo, to be able to look to the cross and to contemplate, from the cross, his city, his diocese, the Church, and the world of his time.

Jesus not only died on the cross for our love, but through his cross, he gave us life. There is no human being on the face of the earth from the beginning to the end of the world that does not owe his or her hope to Christ the Lord.

In this regard, it is useful to recall the words about Jesus, pronounced a few days before his death and also reported by the Evangelist John, when the Jewish leaders were trying to decide whether Jesus should die and were unsure among themselves, with Caiaphas, the high priest, saying that "it was better to have one person die for the people" (John 18:14). The Evangelist adds that these words were prophetic: "Jesus was about to die for the nation, and not for the nation only, but to gather into one the dispersed children of God" (John 11:51–52). This means that Jesus' life is not only offered to those brothers and sisters whom he saw and who were close to him, not even only for the people living in Palestine at that time, but also for people far away, and for all those who in the future will inhabit the world. All of these are called by John "children of God," because God created them in his image and called them to an intimate conversation, even if because of the dark fate of sin they are still far away and unaware of their calling and dignity. It is for all of them, even the most distant, for all the nations, races, and peoples that Jesus dies.

Jesus has redeemed every one of us; his cross is the sign of this universal redemption and the door that opens us to God. Thus, after having spiritually watched with Jesus in the night, hoping to penetrate the mystery of his agony in Gethsemane, after accompanying him in his sorrowful passion that led him to Calvary, we contemplate the wounds and bruises inflicted upon him for our transgressions and iniquities.

I would especially recommend at this point three attitudes for the adoration of Jesus' cross: Lord, we adore you, we thank you, and we believe in you.

We adore you, Lord Jesus, without finding either words or gestures capable of expressing what we think and feel in front of your body broken for our sake, for the sake of humanity. We realize that here, the mystery of the incarnation has reached its climax. By becoming obedient to death, you have revealed that in the world there is a love, God's love, stronger than any sin and stronger than death itself. Thus, the cross is the door through which you enter incessantly in our daily lives. Therefore, we adore you, Lord Jesus, and we thank you, because through your cross, you have become the Lord of our lives and the center that attracts our entire history. Thank you because through your cross, you show your unconditional love, your forgiveness that surrounds us at all times, the intimacy of God the Father, and you become intimate with each one of us as we are, with our sins, with our indifference toward God. You are close to each one of us to awaken in us our most positive energies to be open to the fullness of life. We thank you, and we would like to shout out to all your salvation and your love. We believe because through your cross, we are given the revelation of God as love. The resurrection will only enhance the power of life and love already present in Jesus crucified and risen, who died for love of humanity, a power of life and love that has in no way diminished the suffering, the agony, and the pain of God.

As stated by Miguel de Unamuno, in his poem entitled "The Christ of Velazquez": "You were left alone with your Father, alone in his presence, and your gazes became one, and at the sound of the immense cry coming from your breast the shoreless and bottomless ocean of the Spirit trembled, and God, incarnate in man, tasted the divine loneliness of dying." In silence, we worship all this, we thank you for this, and we believe in this.

An extraordinary word pronounced by Jesus on the cross is *forgiveness*. While they were crucifying him, Jesus raises a prayer to the Father, a prayer that had been long—better yet, always—in his heart: "Father, forgive them; for they do not know what they are doing" (Luke 23:34). All the forgiveness that Jesus offered to Mary Magdalene and many others, the forgiveness that he taught to the disciples and the crowd, it all anticipated that moment when he exclaimed with sorrow and love, "Father, forgive them." And it is because the Father, listening to Jesus' plea, forgives us that we can feel forgiven and forgive others in return. This wonderful last word pronounced by Jesus is the source of all that Jesus keeps forgiving throughout the centuries through the Church, the place of mercy and forgiveness, and particularly through her priests in the sacrament of reconciliation.

This word spoken by Jesus is also the source of the same forgiveness that many martyrs have offered through the power of the Spirit to their killers, from the first martyr Stephen to the many martyrs of our own day. *Forgiveness* is, therefore, the word that should resonate in each of our lives as we are called to invoke both God's forgiveness as well as that of our brothers and sisters whom we have offended; and, in turn, to forgive those who have wronged us as we are called to commit ourselves firmly in the way of love and mercy.

Mary was the first to contemplate the mystery of the cross on Golgotha. We must ask the Mother of God to help us to identify, as she did, with the passion of her Son, to enter into the mystery of his death and the mystery of his life. We must ask her to help us to dwell in his heart, to pray in silence with her and adore the cross, to give thanks, and to believe. We ask Mary to help us to understand, as she did, the mystery of the cross that transforms the entire world and transforms the lives of every man and every woman on earth.

The contemplation of the mystery of the cross is

particularly intense on every Good Friday, but it is also an important component of every eucharistic celebration. Therefore, as I will argue in the following pages, there is profound unity between the mystery of Jesus' passion and the mystery of the Eucharist.

2. JESUS' TESTAMENT

At the Last Supper, his farewell dinner before his death, Jesus pronounced his last words, his last will and testament, as it were; something to be repeated in memory of him. Actually, he leaves not one, but two gestures to repeat in remembrance of him. One is, according to the evangelists Matthew, Mark, and Luke, the breaking of the bread and the distribution of the cup, that is, the Eucharist: "Do this in remembrance of me" (Luke 22:19). The other sign, taught by Jesus in John's Gospel, is mutual service: "So if I, your Lord and Teacher, have washed your feet, you also ought to wash one another's feet" (John 13:14). Thus, both are Jesus' last will and testaments.

Twice, St. Paul in his Letter to the Corinthians, one of the readings for the evening of Holy Thursday according to the Ambrosian rite, after recalling Jesus' words over the bread and wine, repeats Jesus' same exhortation: "Do this, as often as you drink it, in remembrance of me," and "For as often as you eat this bread and drink the cup, you proclaim the Lord's death until he comes" (1 Cor 11:25–26).

During the Last Supper, not only does Jesus become bread to be part of each one of us, but his gift of love expands and multiplies. He says, "Do this in remembrance of me." These words echo those of Mary to the servants at the wedding in Cana: "Do whatever he tells you" (John 2:5). We therefore feel Mary close to us in every Eucharist. She invites us to do what we are commanded by Jesus, to repeat his gestures. Thus, Mary is spiritually present in all the masses that are celebrated around the world, in the great cathedrals, in small towns, in the remotest valleys or mountains. With Mary's intercession, we perceive in every Eucharist something of the holy mystery of God, a mystery of extraordinary beauty and consolation. I therefore invite you to contemplate Jesus as he pronounces the words that we hear repeated during Mass.

In order to grasp more concretely and closely the mystery of the Last Supper, we should consider the words spoken by Jesus during the Consecration of the bread and wine. There is something in Jesus' words that even today fascinates us greatly—the gift of Christ to humanity, Christ, who by his words and gestures, manifests his humanity for us. But we should not forget that Jesus' sign is an enactment of the covenant. Jesus says, "This is my blood of the covenant" (Mark 14:24). This biblical expression recalls the whole history of salvation, God's initiative to be close to humanity with love, starting from Noah and Abraham to Moses. This renewed covenant, recalled by the prophets, is an interpretative category, a ray of light that tears Jesus' gesture from the simple fabric of steadfast human relationships and presents it as the supreme sign of dedication to God in his Son, the sign of tender and faithful love with which God the Father takes care, feeds, frees, forgives, and creates his people.

At the Last Supper, Jesus follows the ritual gestures of the Jewish Passover meal but gives a new and unexpected meaning to them. He breaks the unleavened bread, as was the tradition, but pronounces extraordinary words while doing so: "This is my body" (Luke 22:19), that same body that will be offered for us on the cross. Then he distributes the wine from the cup of blessing as expected, but again, he pronounces an astonishing word while doing so: "This cup that is poured out for you is the new covenant in my blood" (Luke 22:20), that same blood that will be shed on the cross.

3. EUCHARIST AS GIFT OF LIFE

Therefore, at every Eucharist, these mysteries are proclaimed: Jesus' death that destroyed human evil through forgiveness and by overcoming the fear of death. Every Eucharist, then, is for us the fulfillment of the alliance; every Eucharist proclaims the future of man and of humanity; every Eucharist proclaims the day when we will feast with God with whom we will experience an instant familiarity. The Eucharist, instituted at the Last Supper that we commemorate and relive particularly on Holy Thursday, makes ever-present Jesus' Passover and should be understood in this light of alliance and deep acceptance of God's loving will.

The eucharistic meal is expressed in Jesus' gestures: he took the bread, and while blessing it, he broke it and gave it to all; then, he took the cup and had all his disciples drink from it. These words (*bless, break, give*) represent the new way of being, the new way to manage our existence. They embody the centrality of the gratuitousness of the gift, sacrificed and encouraged by God's gratuitousness; by God who is revealed in the Eucharist, who in the eucharistic meal becomes entirely and only love for humanity, love until the end; a steadfast love given to each one of us.

The words that Jesus pronounced over the bread and wine reveal to us his body and his blood as "given for us." Just as when he washed the disciples' feet, he showed his willingness to serve until death, here also, by putting in our hands and mouth the bread and wine, Jesus expresses the totality of his gift, of his life until death. For this reason, in his account the evangelist Matthew goes seamlessly, straight from the Last Supper to Jesus' passion. From the bread, which is Jesus' offered body, and the wine, which is his blood, Matthew goes on to describe immediately the tremendous hour when the Son of Man began to offer his body and shed his blood. For this reason, in the celebration of Holy Thursday, we do not read only the Gospel of the Last Supper but we also begin with the reading of the Gospel of the passion, because Jesus' hour, his death, is already contained in the broken bread and the poured wine.

In this gesture at the Last Supper, there is Jesus' passion and death, his love for us, and all his dedication to humanity; there is the filial spontaneity with which Jesus fulfills the Father's will to the end, his heartfelt acceptance of the mission that must be carried out, overcoming rejection, abandonment, betrayal, passion, and death. Jesus embraces all this with deep filial love, and he proves it by giving his body and his blood to us. Nothing can stop Jesus in his dedication to the Father; neither Judas's betrayal nor Peter's denial, nor the disciples' fleet: none of those situations that so often impede and block us instead in our ability to love.

For this reason, the Eucharist, which is Jesus' ultimate and faithful yes to the Father and to humanity, including his enemies and adversaries, is also for us Christians our way of saying yes to the Father. Our brothers and sisters are not those who show friendship, kindness, and hospitality, but those who do the opposite, that is, those who criticize us, do not accept us, despise us, insult us, and resist us. The Eucharist would be an empty sign if we did not turn into this form of love for others; to be really complete, the Eucharist must be celebrated by us not only as memorial of Jesus' sacrifice, but also in the gift of our lives.

The words reported by St. Paul, "Do this in remembrance of me" (1 Cor 11:24), should not be taken lightly or almost as if they were magical so that it is enough to utter them and then all is done. "Do this in remembrance of me" means especially: "Offer your body as I have offered mine; give yourself even for those who oppose you or do not welcome you as I have done." This is for the Church the true way to celebrate the Eucharist: Jesus opens the way to our offer, to the offer of our bodies as a living sacrifice. It is therefore not only a celebration of a ritual, but it is for us to fully live the totality of our filial gift. Jesus, with his gesture of surrendering himself to us in the washing of the feet and the Eucharist, teaches us to serve, to kneel in front of our brothers and sisters, kneeling in front of everyone, even the most unfriendly and those who betray us, to teach us to offer ourselves to the Father with filial love and in devout obedience. To surrender this way means to have acquired a new mentality that replaces the old one of the prophet Jonah, who considered the people of Nineveh a hopeless cause, who did not want to have anything to do with them, and who wants to avoid a difficult task. It is the Lord who, with much patience, helps him to embrace this mission, the only one that can accomplish the true mystery of salvation.

To offer ourselves this way means to believe in a God who is not angry, bitter, and disappointed by our shortcomings, but who is full of tenderness, trust, and love for every creature; like the Crucified.

Jesus welcomes us to his table knowing that we are, and will be, fragile; perhaps we will betray him; perhaps we will run away. Nonetheless, Jesus breaks the bread for us so that we learn how to do the same with others.

The mystery that we live in every Eucharist is therefore rich in significance. The mystery of Holy Thursday with the Mass of the Lord's Supper can neither be separated from Good Friday nor the Easter Vigil: it is one mystery that unfolds in three days; the mystery of Jesus crucified, buried, and risen; the mystery that is the summit of God's dialogue with us; the mystery that is the source of all Christian life, the life of the Church, and of all feasts of the liturgical year.

All the events and mysteries, from the night of Jesus' agony in Gethsemane to the crucifixion, to Jesus' death, until the cold night in the tomb and the bright night of the resurrection, are summed up in the one mystery of the Eucharist, in front of which we are called to lower our heads to adore Jesus in the depths and the silence of our hearts. At the Last Supper, Jesus, in fact, put a seal on the story of his long love by delivering himself to death; a love that no betrayal was able to stop, no cock's crow could prevent. Jesus' hour, the hour that was a sum of all the hours of his life and of human history, the hour of the supreme, total, free gift of himself, is contained in the Eucharist and anticipates, summarizes, and contains everything.

The evening of Holy Thursday is in fact the time when Jesus, with the signs of the broken bread and the poured wine, anticipates the heart-rending sacrifice of the cross, which took place once and for all on Calvary. Thus, Jesus ensures in a concrete way through the

Eucharist, the tangible and mysterious permanence of his death on the cross for us, of his supreme love for humanity, of his coming into us to save and sanctify us. In the Eucharist itself are enclosed all the events that happened after the Last Supper: from Jesus' agony to his passion, crucifixion, and death; from the cold night in the tomb to the radiant morning of the resurrection. In his obedience, Jesus faithfully sums up all that the Father has asked of him to do for the salvation of the world and summarizes his unconditional dedication that does not falter in front of the betrayals of Judas and our own, nor in front of Peter's denial and our own inconsistencies. His heart, which on the cross will be torn apart, already starts to open during the Last Supper to pour the Spirit on the Church and the world.

All the Gospels place the episode of the Last Supper before the long account of Jesus' passion except John who, instead, introduces the account of the washing of the disciples' feet.

Through this arrangement, the evangelists show the close relationship that exists between the Last Supper, Jesus' ultimate gesture of love, and his passion: the Last Supper is therefore the key to understand what will eventually happen as it explains the deeper meaning of Jesus' death and resurrection; it is also a principle of perennial relevance for everything that we do in the Eucharist. In the Lord's Supper, we receive the concrete way, which Jesus wanted, to make his Passover perennially present in the life of the Church and human history. Jesus himself, as it is clear from his words during the Last Supper, indicated the sense that his death—faced with love and out of love for us—would assume and left us the meaning of his death in the Eucharist.

Even in the passage from the First Letter of St. Paul to the Corinthians, the apostle hands down to us what he himself received, that is, Jesus on the night that he was betrayed took the bread, broke it, and said, "This is my body that is for you" (11:24). The broken bread, which is Christ himself, is inseparable from his broken body on the cross. Thus, the Eucharist is the proclamation of the Lord's death until he comes again, and every Mass we celebrate allows us to pass from death to life, from this world to the Father, powerfully drawing us to God where we will eternally celebrate the feast of the messianic joy. Further, the bread that we break is Jesus' flesh for the life of the world. The Eucharist surpasses all boundaries and stands as judgment on history and on the ability of Jesus' disciples to be in him a sign of unity and love. Therefore, the Mass that we celebrate opens us to the world; it becomes a mission, a loving passion of the Church for the salvation of humanity.

The words that Jesus spoke over the bread and wine during the Last Supper are words that never cease to surprise us, to move us, to amaze us; they are words that produce in the world something similar to an explosion of love that nothing and nobody will ever be able to stop and that reaches us today, like burning lava, when we celebrate the Eucharist. Not even death will end the love given to us by Jesus; nothing can eradicate from the world this divine fire of love that burns but does not consume and reaches us in the Eucharist. In it, in fact, the miracle of Christ's love, which becomes our food and our drink, emphasizes and symbolizes the ultimate redeeming sacrifice that took place on Calvary. The Eucharist continues to feed humanity with the Christian law of love. By receiving the body and blood of Jesus, our lives become part of his destiny, death, and resurrection. For this we are invited to approach the bread and wine with fear and trembling; in the Eucharist, our heart becomes one with the heart of Jesus, and his heart makes ours his own.

The Eucharist, as symbol of food and nourishment, reveals that Jesus wants to be with us, identify with us, live in us, give himself to us, lead us to the mystical union with him, that is, the union of wills, the fusion of two hearts who love each other. The Eucharist reveals the infinity of God's love, mercy, tenderness for each one of us. Therefore, the Eucharist, through its symbols, expresses Jesus' desire to give everything to us, as he gave himself to us on the cross.

In the eucharistic communion, Jesus gives himself to us and makes us part of him to the extent that our heart is undivided, and we give up ourselves to accept to become children of God in Jesus and brothers and sisters of every person. Jesus gives himself to us to the extent that we love one another and we serve one another as he has commanded us to do after washing the disciples' feet.

In the Eucharist, Jesus offers himself to us, he gives himself to us in his body and blood. He teaches us to let ourselves be loved, forgiven, and showered with gifts from something that looks smaller and more fragile than ourselves. He teaches us to love one another, to offer our bodies and our lives for one another as he has done for us.

Therefore, let us contemplate the Eucharist as the marvelous image of God's weakness and powerlessness, of God's being a friend to humanity. We contemplate the Eucharist from a position of weakness that is, to a certain extent, close even to the so-called contemporary "weak thought" that shies away from rigid and inflexible systems and in the presence of the splendor of being. Well, God in the Eucharist is not inflexible; God did not appear in the splendor of glory but, as St. Paul says, he emptied himself, he became little and rejected so that we could be won over by his humbling and vulnerable love.

The Eucharist is therefore nourishment for our weakness: we are weaker than Peter and Jonah, whose stories are narrated in the Scriptures, and Jesus himself takes the form of weakness under the species of bread and wine to feed us and to make us stronger. Among other things, this gesture has ethical implications as it reveals what is at the heart of the moral experience of love, of renouncing to self and its interests, acknowledging the primacy of the gift and the free exchange of what one has and of what one is. Therefore, the Eucharist reveals the heart of our moral experience, the leaving behind of self, the free gift of oneself.

Thus, to put at the center the Eucharist means to be invited to a more vivid Christian experience around the eucharistic table, starting from a renewed commitment to the inner life that culminates in a more generous expression of charity. With the certainty that we are called to create living communities of faith—even in modern and urban settings—around the mystery of the Eucharist, we must in particular ask our Lord Jesus to help us take the broken bread and the poured wine, his body and his blood, to the world. We must bring Jesus into all our communities so that the Eucharist is truly the center of all our endeavors. Let us ask Jesus to help us to bring that offering that is inscribed in the gift of his body and blood; the offering of mercy, of tenderness, of service, of becoming neighbors; the offering of a burning passion to every suffering creature, so that they may become communities that continually receive their nourishment and their joy from the eucharistic meal. We must, therefore, ask Jesus to always help us recognize him in the Eucharist; to recognize him as we ourselves become broken bread, living bread in the darkness of this world. Let us pray to Jesus to give us that fire, that passionate love for the Father that led him to hand over his life, to empty himself for the salvation of us all.

4. *YOU ALSO SHOULD DO AS I HAVE DONE TO YOU*

The Eucharist is the sacrifice of the new covenant, as Jesus said, in the words reported by St. Paul: "This cup is the new covenant in my blood" (1 Cor 11:25).

The term "covenant" here recalls Moses' covenant on Sinai and Moses' covenant included what we call the Ten Commandments, the law of the covenant: there is in fact no covenant without a law that guarantees the compliance with the terms of that same covenant. What is then the law of the eucharistic covenant, the covenant of the bread and wine? This law is symbolically expressed by Matthew, Mark, and Luke and is explicitly expressed by John who, in the context of the Last Supper, recounts how Jesus did not only say, "You also ought to wash one another's feet" (John 13:14), which means, serve one another, but also, "Just as I have loved you, you also should love one another" (John 13:34). These words are reported by John after the description of the washing of the disciples' feet. The two signs, the broken bread and poured wine and the washing of the feet, recall each other; they both want to express Jesus' love, his total dedication to us, and God's love for humanity. Both want to give us the example, the stimulus, and the grace of brotherly love.

Further, both the gesture of the bread and wine and the washing of the feet recall the purification from sins: Jesus' blood is shed for the purification from sins, and the washing of the disciples' feet is performed so they are completely purified.

Thus, there is a parallel between the institution of the Eucharist, as told in the Gospels of Matthew, Mark, and Luke, and also mentioned by St. Paul, and the story of the washing of the feet transmitted by John. The Fourth Evangelist in fact does not offer an account of the institution of the Eucharist, but in reporting Jesus' Last Supper, he recounts the washing of the disciples' feet, the same gesture that bishops repeat at the beginning of the celebration of Holy Thursday. Exegetes have always wondered why John omitted the account of the institution of the Eucharist and put in its place the washing of the disciples' feet. Apart from other reasons that perhaps we do not know that well, one thing is absolutely clear: John deliberately placed this gesture of service, that is, the "washing of the disciples' feet" performed by Jesus, Lord and Teacher, on the same level with the gesture of the bread and wine, distributed to the disciples at the Last Supper, as Jesus' body and blood.

A careful reading of the two stories, that of the washing of the feet in John and the institution of the Eucharist in Matthew, Mark, Luke, and Paul, allows us to grasp the allusions and similarities (starting from the identical location) between the two episodes that at first glance, may seem unrelated.

This mysterious text about Jesus washing the disciples' feet, considered a fundamental moment in the Easter mystery, is a Gospel passage rich in meaning. Jesus performs here an enigmatic gesture: he washes the disciples' feet. It is a gesture that raises some questions, such as, "What and why are you doing this?" and it also gives the opportunity for a lesson. It is therefore a gesture very suited to Jesus' behavior and also to the didactic practice of Jewish transmission of tradition and rabbinic teaching: it represents a fact that raises a question that in turn can be answered.

We could also argue whether it was just a gesture of friendship and almost of gratitude toward his close friends. After all, Jesus praises his disciples for their loyalty. In fact, he tells them during that dinner, "You are those who have stood by me in my trials" (Luke 22:28). But the passage in chapter 13 of John's Gospel recounting the washing of the feet communicates much more. In it, we have learned to read not only an act of service or courtesy toward friends, but the willingness of the same Son of God to give his life for humanity.

The passage describes the way in which Jesus washed the feet of his disciples: a menial task and one that Jesus did not usually perform; for that very reason, it takes on an extraordinary importance. It is customary to give an account of this task in a very simple way, saying, "Jesus teaches that we must serve one another." This is certainly true; Jesus himself said, "So if I, your Lord and Teacher, have washed your feet, you also ought to wash one another's feet" (John 13:14). But this statement should not be taken simply in a material sense: in his life, Jesus performed this gesture only once, not every day; he did not claim that it was a material gesture to be repeated almost mechanically. It is a symbolic gesture by which Jesus is not simply saying, "Humbly serve one another," but it wants to convey more fully, "I put my life at your disposal, I give my life for you."

Further, Jesus, as the full expression of God's divinity, and aware of the fullness of his powers, by washing the feet of his disciples, overturns our false image of God, gives a new meaning to our notion of freedom, and teaches us the perfection of love.

Thus, these are the true meanings of the washing of the feet that therefore derive from this profound intention of Jesus: the washing of the disciples' feet is a prophetic gesture, which also provides the key to understanding Jesus' life and imminent death. In the washing of the feet, we reflect on how much God loves humanity to the point of serving us and offering Christ for our salvation.

The washing of the disciples' feet is placed at the center of John's account of the Last Supper. It is not a simple, marginal episode; rather, John puts it in place of the Eucharist: it is an important sign that represents a message that in John replaces the message of the eucharistic meal. For this reason, the washing of the disciples' feet is also a way of describing the Eucharist that John does not mention. In Jesus' gestures, we read the offering he makes of himself and his life for the love of humanity: the laying down of his garments stands for the laying down of his life; the washing of the feet for Jesus' taking upon himself of the role of slave until the final moment of his death; just as putting his clothes back on symbolizes the retaking of his glorious body in his resurrection. It is therefore a sign exceptionally rich in meaning: God serves humanity in Jesus to the point of offering his life for our salvation, and then regaining it back through the glory of his resurrection.

The gesture of the washing of the disciples' feet is the gesture that Jesus performs first; it is the same gesture that the bishop repeats at the beginning of the celebration of the Mass *in Coena Domini* on Holy Thursday; it is the gesture that for Jesus means the gift of himself, of his service, of his life, and of his death.

This gesture is at the heart of all Jesus' acts and gestures during the Last Supper: the offering of his body and blood; the words of love for his disciples; the prolonged discourse after the Supper; the agony in Gethsemane; the encounter with his traitor; the standing trial; the enduring of Peter's denial: everything that we hear and meditate during the liturgy of the Holy Week. Jesus' gesture of the washing of the feet signifies and includes everything else: it is the place from which we can contemplate, starting from our conscience and from the awareness of Christ, all the unfolding of the mysteries of Jesus' passion, beginning with the gift of the Eucharist. This fundamental gesture is the source from which we can experience the awareness with which Christ goes toward his passion, and it is also the gesture that is at the root of the awareness of the Church, the awareness that the Church has of herself, the awareness that the Church has of being Christ's Church and of being the Church of her Lord.

5. CHURCH MEANS TO SERVE

Jesus kneels down in front of each man and woman to wash their feet because every person is a child of God, and all are called to be one people, one entity, one body with one another and in Jesus; everybody is called to be, with Jesus, children of the one Father who is in heaven.

What I have written so far leads us now to reflect, at least indirectly, on the close ties that exist between the Eucharist, the eucharistic table, the eucharistic sacrifice, the consecration of the bread and wine, and the humble service of our brothers and sisters; in short, the relationship between the Eucharist and charity. We are particularly encouraged to reflect on the relationship between the Eucharist and charity starting from the concrete gesture that the bishop performs at the beginning of the celebration of the Mass *in Coena domini*, on Holy Thursday, that is, the washing of the feet, which often involves some of the brothers and sisters from among those who live where there is a more imperative and urgent need of good neighbors and service. The question then is to see how the Eucharist and compassionate service are related to each other.

Regarding the relationship between the Eucharist and charity, it is useful to ask ourselves what the Eucharist says about the service of mutual love of Christians among themselves and between Christians and all other people. The Eucharist tells us that charity is the fundamental attitude of those who have let themselves be attracted by Jesus. Before being an act, an initiative, a program, charity is a spiritual attitude; a merciful unity of intent with Jesus dying on the cross; an entering into the heart of the eucharistic Christ and letting ourselves be captivated by his love that drives us.

Second, the Eucharist, as a memorial of the cross (What is the Eucharist if we forget Easter, that is, Jesus' death on the cross and his resurrection?), proclaims the reality of love: love and the service to others points to the resurrection, that is, they point to rehabilitation and recovery, just as Jesus' death leads to the resurrection. But Jesus' service of love develops, first of all, in the brave acceptance of pain, suffering, weakness, even apparent defeat. Therefore, considerate love that originates from the Eucharist and has as its model Jesus' washing of the disciples' feet is a love that overcomes the reality of evil, but not eluding, sidestepping, or marginalizing it; rather, by penetrating it.

The person who, in order to face so much evil in the world, claimed or expected to see an immediate and fully satisfactory outcome of one's efforts, in the illusion of not having to face any dangers, discomfort, nor defeat, would only be condemned to serious delusions and would not follow Jesus' love, which, above all, means to go toward the cross.

Thus, the love that springs from Jesus' death and resurrection, that is, from the Eucharist, is a strong love of steadfast hope, even in the face of dangers and defeats; a love that knows that there are no irreparable situations. This love brings about many healing communities; many acts of courage toward people in extreme difficulties; many recoveries in people who seemed hopeless even in their own eyes, but who, in the face of this new openness of hope, feel reborn even in suffering and in pain.

Third, the compassionate charity that arises from the Eucharist teaches us also whom we need to direct our attention toward today, that is, to those who most need the certainty of the love of Easter. Hence, the charity of our communities, when it really comes from the Eucharist, looks for every person suffering for any reason: every sick or marginalized person—every drug addict, HIV-positive person, or inmate—to tell them that even their condition can give rise to a germ of love; to assure them that if they can believe in love or make some small, loving gesture, they have found the way to salvation.

In particular, we can refer to the fact, known to all, that in our cities, there is an increasingly intense foreign presence, especially of immigrants from developing countries. As a result, more and more complex reactions emerge, and discussions, surveys, positions multiply; we can also run into attitudes and episodes that reveal reactions ranging from worried, irritated, negative, to those of closure toward the presence of African or Asian foreigners in Italy. In effect, when in Italy and generally speaking in Central Europe, the number of foreign presences exceeded the minimum limit. It revealed that under an apparent attitude of acceptance, good humor, and kindness, there lurked, even for us Italians, a real struggle to accept those who come from far away, and who then appear as those who threaten our peace and our stability. But as citizens, we have an obligation to take a stand in front of episodes that, in their intolerance, are a violation of the democratic spirit and fabric. The values of solidarity and respect that are present in our Constitution and in our legislation cannot be disregarded and contradicted in substance: can the same people whose ancestors have personally suffered the hardships of emigration express toward those arriving in Italy attitudes of closure and rejection?

But the resurgent phenomenon of intolerance toward those who are of a different race or color challenges us not only as citizens, but above all, as Christians. We are encouraged by the power of the Gospel to proclaim and practice hospitality, reconciliation, solidarity toward all. We are urged to proclaim our vocation; to know how to be one people. Looking at Jesus washing the feet of his disciples, we can re-read many other episodes in which Jesus praises or supports someone who is not of his race or his people: he praises the Samaritan, the only one of the ten lepers who returned to thank him; he praises the centurion, a pagan, and the stranger who takes care of the wounded. Jesus will tell us in the Last Judgment: "I was a stranger and you welcomed me," but also "Truly I tell you, just as you did not do it to one of the least of these, you did not do it to me" (Matt 25:35, 45).

If, therefore, the last represent the humanity worthy of being served by Jesus himself with his own hands, the priorities are already categorically laid down by him. So Jesus washes our feet and gives himself to us in the Eucharist to convert the way we think about God and our brothers and sisters. When we eat the consecrated bread, Jesus says to us, "Do this, become yourself broken bread, given to your brothers and sisters." Therefore, we should offer ourselves to the serving of others; kneel not only for ten minutes after communion, but in real life in serving those in need; this is what it means to return to a spirit that is humble, fraternal, evangelical, capable of acceptance.

Surrendering oneself to others means to open up to a new attitude, just as the prophet Jonah is obliged to do; an attitude that reflects the mercy of God who loves all people around the world.

An ecclesiological consequence of the Eucharist is the one that is expressed in the ancient rite of the washing of the feet. The Church's mission is to serve; the Church is for others; the Church is there to give all of herself, just as Jesus became a servant for our love. In the liturgy of Holy Thursday, we perform this symbolic gesture of the washing of the feet, which truly is symbolically fulfilled, because we know well that we do not live it in practice. We perform this symbolic gesture even to say that we would like to live it in practice, but we are far from being able to do that; thus, we ask for God's mercy and conversion because, in reality, only in words do we profess charity, service, solidarity, even if at times and in different ways, we do so also in deeds. But when charity and service really require the gift of life, then we feel rising from the depths of ourselves a repugnance and myriad excuses and pretexts; when charity requires something serious, we are content to watch Jesus washing the disciples' feet, but we instinctively pull back.

6. HE LOVES US UNTO THE END

All the mysteries of Jesus' life, the whole history of salvation, all the pages of the Scriptures express nothing but the passionate love of God for our humanity, and Jesus' passion is the culmination of this revelation.

On the evening of Holy Thursday, we commemorate Jesus' Last Supper, during which he has given us some of the most extraordinary signs of his love: he gave his body and his blood for us as a sign of the gift of his life in his passion and death, he has called us friends, and he washed the disciples' feet. Therefore, the liturgy of the Mass *in Coena Domini* on Holy Thursday is extremely rich in symbols, gestures, and meanings. However, all these symbols, gestures, and meanings express one great mystery: the amazing love of God for humanity.

This love is shown in particular in the mystery of the Eucharist—it is of this amazing love that I wrote about at the beginning of my pastoral letter of 1996, *Restarting from God*, when I evoked the thrill of fear I felt holding in my hands the monstrance with the consecrated bread during the Corpus Christi procession on the Navigli canals in Milan: "I contemplate the Lord Jesus and feel a thrill go through me at the sight of his vulnerability. Here he is, praised by many people, yet he is weak and allows us to handle him as we please. We could do anything to him, and he would not react, just as he did during his passion: this is the Lord of Hosts, the Almighty."

Thus, precisely this mystery of vulnerability, of glory in weakness, of endless love is what we contemplate the evening of Holy Thursday at its source, that is, at the institution of the Eucharist during the Last Supper.

The Ambrosian rite for Holy Thursday has traditionally three fixed readings that are interrelated to better help us understand the mystery celebrated during this solemnity. The first reading presents us with the finding that the mystery of God on Nineveh is so unfathomable that not even the prophet Jonah, despite the fact that he had gone through many trials, had been educated in so many ways, reprimanded, warned, and illuminated by God, understood this mystery. Jonah did not want to preach to the city because he had the feeling that God's word to the city was one of curse and condemnation, and he was afraid to have any part in that. But when he finally decided to preach to the city, to call its people to repentance with the threat of destruction, and then saw that God's mercy is much bigger than he had thought, he closed in on himself and was saddened.

The story of Jonah reminds us of God's tenderness, faithfulness, and mercy that find their ultimate expression in Jesus' Passover.

Jonah is each one of us who cannot recognize the greatness of the mercy of God—the power of the sign of the cross over our own cities—each one of us who tends to be mistrustful and fearful, whose heart and spirit is distressed over our cities that are not any worse than Nineveh; these cities that have great potentials for love and giving, not only those of ancient and present times, but also those of the future. Each one of us is called to enlarge our hearts to measure God's mercy, not according to Jonah's small-mindedness and fear or his flights and his reluctance, but with a boundless confidence in the mystery of God's mercy and love.

This mystery of love and mercy, as seen in the second reading from the Letter of St. Paul to the Corinthians, is a mystery of sharing; a mystery in which everyone is called to come out of one's shell—from one's comfortable life—to leave aside what could be eaten alone in one's home and join the common banquet; to join in the joy of sharing around the one table of Christ.

These words bring to mind those of St. Charles Borromeo, who once said to the city of Milan in one of his famous admonitions, from one of his biographies, "People of Milan, look to the rock from which you were cut, and to the quarry from which you were hewn; rethink back on the roots of the fruits that you see among you; cultivate them, embrace them. Someone will certainly say, 'I take communion often but remain cold or lukewarm; I can hardly recognize my blessings'; but that is precisely the fruit: recognize your coldness, this infirmity of yours; and who better could remove it from you more effectively if not the grace and the giver of grace, that is, Christ? What was Christ for the primitive Church is the Eucharist for us. The power is the same as well: you will receive the same fruits."

The third reading, the Gospel recounting the Last Supper, by speaking of the fulfillment of this plan of mercy within the city, despite Peter and the disciples' lack of understanding, despite the opposition and rejection of the powerful in Jerusalem, comforts us as we look at the cross of Christ and his Eucharist as a sign of victory for today. Nothing, neither the human misunderstanding and obtuseness of the disciples themselves, nor the open or devious opposition of enemies and opponents, nor the indifference of those who pass by and look away, nothing can stand against the power of the merciful cross of Christ over the city; nothing can stand against us, who are the first to receive from the Eucharist this message and are called to translate it into our daily lives and announce it to all with missionary zeal, because the days of grace of Holy Week and Easter are days of grace for all our cities.

Therefore, on the evening of Holy Thursday, the readings and the washing of the feet that is ritually performed invite us to contemplate first merciful love of God who in Jesus overcomes every obstacle to come in this hour to meet every man and woman. Second, we are invited to reflect on the different human responses to this merciful love of God, in the hour of Gethsemane, of death, of resurrection, of Eucharist.

First, then, we are invited to contemplate God's merciful love, and we do so both in the three readings of the Mass and in the washing of the feet that, for this reason, reveal four images of God's merciful love: God wants to forgive the city of Nineveh, the corrupt and lost city, but God wants to forgive her because he loves her (reading from the Book of Jonah); God admonishes and corrects the Corinthian community that does not understand the deeper meaning of the Eucharist (reading from the Letter to the Corinthians); Jesus serves the disciples and washes their feet to show his love unto the end (the gesture of the washing of the feet that is performed during the celebration with reference to chapter 13 of John's Gospel). Finally, Jesus accepts Judas's kiss of betrayal because he wants to give his love even to those who betray him and deny him (the story of the passion).

Therefore, these four icons, these four messages reveal the only way God knows how to deal with us, that is, with infinite merciful love, and all four are expressed in the Eucharist, in the sign of the broken bread and poured wine. But if these are the ways, and the only way, of God's merciful love for us who are ungrateful, forgetful, careless, then how do we respond? How does man react to these offers of love and salvation from the part of God? An answer can be seen in the same four characters mentioned in the readings and gestures that we have already mentioned: Jonah, the faithful of Corinth, Judas, and Peter.

The first is Jonah who did not want to hear the call to be the "herald of God's mercy," who did not want to deal with people that he considered corrupt and lost; therefore, he flew away from the Lord. Jonah did not understand a God who saves sinners; a God who loves not only the good but also the bad does not befit him. That God did not match the image that Jonah had created of God. Through his story, we realize that Jonah's conversion to the true image of God is almost more difficult than the conversion of the poor people of Nineveh who cannot distinguish right from wrong.

Even the faithful of Corinth resist the gift of God; they do not recognize the immense gift of the Eucharist they have in their hands. For them, it is perhaps something too simple; perhaps they would have liked the Eucharist to be something more beautiful, whose efficacy was more tangible, more triumphant, thus they lose the sense of the small, humble signs given by Jesus in the bread and wine and end up divided and fighting among themselves. The Lord, with love, rebukes them, corrects them so they understand that Jesus' offer of his body and his blood is under humble signs: a great mystery that requires from us that we welcome one another with love.

Even Peter, during the washing of the feet, protests when Jesus performs this act of humble service and would not want his feet to be washed. Peter in effect is refusing Jesus' passion; it is a reaction that we ourselves can have: it is hard to be loved, to be served by God, who for love dies on the cross. Peter would rather do something himself for the Lord, something great, serving his master to see him eventually triumph, but Jesus only asks him to let himself be loved; it is what Jesus asks us in the Eucharist as well.

Our true condition of children is precisely to be second in love to God, who first loved us even when we did not exist, when we were without merit, when we were sinners. Thus, it is a matter of recognizing our being creatures, our condition of children, saved and forgiven.

Finally, in the last reading of the passion, we contemplate the horrible mystery of Judas's betrayal. Judas was totally disappointed by Jesus; he had followed him, but he hoped for some social and political greatness for his people, and ended up betraying Jesus because he, in turn, felt betrayed. Jesus was not the man he had hoped for; the kingdom of which Jesus speaks is not that great and amazing kingdom that he was waiting for. Judas, therefore, refused to be loved by Jesus as Jesus would have liked to love him.

Thus, these are the four attitudes of the divine initiative of salvation with respective forms of human resistance as seen in Jonah, the faithful of Corinth, Peter, and Judas. These forms of resistance represent our struggle to really understand the mystery of the

Eucharist and to enter with ease and openness into Holy Week, letting Jesus love us.

Still, in front of these four characters we find Jesus, whose behavior can be summarized in one sentence spoken by the Fourth Evangelist to describe what Jesus did in the washing of the feet, that is, "he loved them to the end" (John 13:1). Although Jonah, the Corinthians, Peter, and Judas oppose resistance, Jesus loved them to the end by giving up his life. These words, "he loved them to the end," summarize and explain the way God acts, his leaning down with love for humanity. "To the end" means to the maximum depth and until the very end. In its simplicity and brevity, this expression reaches the heights, reaches the very heart of the mystery of salvation, makes us touch the trinitarian mystery. In John's language, the expression "he loved them to the end" announces Jesus' passion, the infinite love of the Son who, in obedience to the Father, will humble himself to death on the cross. "He loved them to the end": this expression combines love and humbling, perfect love and total lowering of self. Two realities that are present in the Eucharist and inseparably united in all the gestures of Christ's redemption. Two realities, love and humbling, which have, in some mysterious way, their roots in the Trinity itself.

The Gospel of the passion speaks first of the assumptions of this fact and then describes it in its happening, to communicate its meanings. The assumption is expressed with very solemn words: "Jesus knew that his hour had come to depart from this world and go to the Father. Having loved his own who were in the world, he loved them to the end" (John 13:1). Immediately, we grasp the solemn, momentous implication of these words: "Jesus knew" expresses Jesus' full awareness—the awareness that his hour had come, the hour of which Jesus spoke about with his Blessed Mother Mary, at the wedding at Cana: "My hour has not yet come" (John 2:4). Now, instead, is the time and the time of passing "from this world to the Father." This formula indicates in the most complete and comprehensive fashion the whole mystery of Christ and of Easter. It is not just the passion, death, and resurrection; it is not simply the liberation of humanity; rather, it is Jesus' passing from this world to the Father, together with all those who believe in him, to bring us to a deified life, to bring us into the fullness of God's kingdom in the sharing of the very life of God.

A word in Jesus' life and passion has always struck me powerfully: the "hour." In the Gospel we read on Holy Thursday, it seems to be applied to Jesus' enemies.

He says, "But this is your hour" (Luke 22:53). However, the same word appears in other moments in the Gospels where it refers to Jesus. It is mentioned as "his hour had come to depart from this world and go to the Father" (John 13:1); "the hour has come; the Son of Man is betrayed into the hands of sinners" (Mark 14:41); "the hour has come for the Son of Man to be glorified" (John 12:23). It ultimately represents the hour of Jesus' free offering of himself. Jesus, who at birth was entrusted to the hands of Mary, who at the Presentation in the Temple is entrusted to the hands of Simeon, on Holy Thursday freely offers himself to the hands of his friends, and on Good Friday he is delivered in the hands of his executioners and through all of this he will offer himself eternally on the cross to the hands of the Father. It is, therefore, the hour of Jesus' giving up his life, the hour of his offering it to the Father. In the hour when he washes the disciples' feet, Jesus asks us to put ourselves at the service of one another. The episode of Jesus washing his disciples' feet is not simply a gesture of humble service, the service that servants used to render to their masters. Jesus put himself on the side of the last, and teaches us to do the same, but not only that. With this gesture, in the context in which it is performed and with the words with which the evangelist describes it, Jesus symbolically declares that he wants to give his life for his own: to be willing to give his life for his friends; it is what Jesus declares in the act of breaking bread and passing the cup. "This is my body, which is given for you.…This cup that is poured out for you is the new covenant in my blood" (Luke 22:19, 20). If Jesus praised the widow who gives everything she has, the woman who breaks open the precious vase of pure nard, and Mary who wastes for him three-hundred denarii, it is because these gestures of love, these unconditional gifts, are primarily a reflection of himself, an image of the Father, a window opened on the ocean of giving that is the Trinity.

Contemplating Jesus washing his disciples' feet, we also contemplate our own mystery: we are here to be loved, to let ourselves be loved, to let our feet be washed by Jesus, to let us be forgiven and cleansed by the Word, and to let ourselves be loved by someone who does not want to love us as from above, almost as if dropping us a gift from heaven, but from the lowest level, that is, putting himself at our service.

This hour of which the Gospel speaks is, therefore, vast and rich; it is also realized in every Eucharist in which Jesus is in our hands to help us get through the fear of death and reach the certainty that we are already united to him, already here in this life and on earth, to make us understand how to live in an attitude of service and gift of ourselves to others, to make us able to love and to forgive, to enable us to transform, in him and with him, the world and return it to the Father.

With the aforementioned premise to the story of Jesus' passion, the evangelist wants to emphasize Jesus' serenity and authority in performing the last, simplest, and most humble gestures of his life, in preparing himself to face his dark, cruel, tragic fate that awaits him: Jesus lives all this with full consciousness, with total peace of mind, in emotional communion with God's will, without anxiety and without fear because he is totally entrusting himself to the Father. In this context of emotions, feelings, and foreboding, Jesus loves his own and, after having loved them, "loves them to the end." Even this simple word *love* allows us to read and re-read Jesus' whole life, the whole mystery of God: love means "to want the other to be"; to love means "to let the other be, let the other grow and become first"; loving also means "to let the other be even at one's own expense, at the cost of self-sacrifice, of one's life." All this occurs here, for us, in Jesus: he loves us to the end, that is, until the very end, that is, to the point of dying for us, to fill up the measure of love.

The Eucharist is above all the revelation of the Father's love, of his will to be in a covenant with humanity today, right now. It is the revelation of the Father through the total dedication to the Father Jesus lived and that creates and reinforces in us the will to renounce to ourselves to belong fully to the Father. Jesus says, "This is my blood of the covenant, which is poured out for many" (Mark 14:24). This biblical word "covenant" recalls all the initiative of God's love for man, from Noah to Abraham and Moses, and through the centuries. Every time that the Eucharist is celebrated, the whole history of salvation is summarized and flows into eternity. Thanks to the Eucharist, humanity, divided and scattered, gradually becomes one in Christ. In every Eucharist, we are invited to ask ourselves what is the Father revealing to me today of himself, of his boundless love for me. What does he reveal of who I am, of my being made to love and forgive with Christ and like Christ? What does he tell me of the other men and women who are waiting for this love and this gift?

In the context of the Last Supper, therefore, Jesus' most humble and simple gesture of the washing of the feet, his gesture of offering himself in the bread and wine expresses his intimate disposition of wanting to love unto the end, to be faithful to God who serves humanity. With the Eucharist and the washing of the feet, Jesus invites his disciples to understand the meaning of his death and urges us to wash each other's feet, that is, to move from faith to action, from understanding to practical life. What Jesus does in the Eucharist, therefore, coincides with his ability to love humanity to the point of giving his life for us, to push his human freedom to the point of loving as the Father loves us, to forgive as God forgives us, to be faithful to us as God is faithful, to be forbearing and patient as the Father is to see us, his friends, free, and to see even his enemies free; just as the Father creates, he wants and lets us be free.

It is, therefore, up to us not to receive this mystery of love in vain; it is up to us to participate in the Lord's Supper with that attitude of conversion mentioned in the Book of Jonah: the conversion of the sinful city of Nineveh, but also the conversion of the prophet Jonah, called to accept God's merciful initiative for sinners.

This is the message of the eucharistic celebration. Thus, in front of this message, we must ask ourselves, can we really respond to this love until the end? Are we able to let ourselves be loved this way, and will we be able, in the wake of this love, to love until the end while immersed in conflicts, contradictions, uncertainties, and the ordinariness of the world and society? In the Eucharist, Jesus has set the perennial sign of this love *to the end*, and the Eucharist continues to remind us of this love and to put it in our hearts. To love, therefore, to the end is to be loved by the Eucharist, and to love in the power of the Eucharist.

How can we concretely offer to the world this love that stems from the Eucharist? We are called, with our serene and unyielding manner of doings things in everyday life, to proclaim that life has meaning, that life is not an absurd and blind adventure because, as Pope John Paul II wrote in his encyclical *Evangelium Vitae*, "The revelation of the Gospel of life is given to us as a good to be shared with all people: so that all men and women may have fellowship with us and with the Trinity. Our own joy would not be complete if we failed to share this Gospel with others but kept it only for ourselves."

Christ Is Risen from the Dead

1. A HISTORICAL EVENT THAT CHANGES HISTORY

The word *Easter* had in antiquity and throughout the centuries different resonances and thus different liturgical embodiments: Easter means first "God's passing over" and then the work of God who saves; it means people's passing from slavery to freedom; it also means Jesus' passion; and finally, his passing to the Father that sums up the whole of the paschal mystery. Among these four meanings, it is especially the third one that is underscored by the liturgy of Holy Week, that is, Easter as "passion," corresponding to the medieval etymology that was given to the Greek word *pascha*, by relating it to the Greek word *paschein* (to grieve; to suffer); thus, this word was primarily interpreted in relation to Jesus' "suffering." A suffering that is certainly Jesus' passage to the Father, which in turn is God's redeeming passage through humanity as well as the passing from death to life, from slavery to freedom, from sin to grace.

The Easter we celebrate every year is first of all the memory of a historical event; thus, it is not simply an ideal commemoration or meditation on some abstract reality; it is the memory of an event, a specific one that is historically well-defined: namely, Jesus' trial conducted by the Roman authorities that ended with his death sentence, torture, and crucifixion and, a few days after Jesus' death, with the historical record of the meeting of the risen Christ with his disciples.

The Gospel that we hear during the celebration of the Easter Vigil is about a mysterious event that is proclaimed with the following words: Jesus of Nazareth "has been raised from the dead" (Matt 28:7). But this event is contained in the mystery of God; it is an event that is neither described nor told; it is only proclaimed: it is part of the mystery of God, of the mystery of the Son, and of the mystery of the Holy Spirit. However, there are signs pointing to this mysterious event, realities through which it is made manifest. These realities, in Matthew's Gospel, are the earthquake, the lightning, the angels' words; these will be followed by the appearances of Jesus himself and his own meeting with the apostles, who will testify to the great mystery they have witnessed.

Through all this manifestation of the mystery of Christ's glory in the historical realities of this world, of our history, of our life, it is usually said that this mysterious and astonishing fact of Jesus' resurrection is something that undoubtedly is part of the mystery of God, the mystery of Christ, and of Christ's glory, but this mystery of God, of Christ, and of Christ's glory appears, is made present, bursts into our own history. It is the irruption in our history of God's loving power that creates and recreates life. The same powerful irruption of God in history described in chapter 1 of the Book of Genesis, through which life is given to the world, is repeated here with the fullness of the power of God that gives life back to Christ, who lies dead in the tomb and, in him, gives life to the world.

This event that is announced by the Gospel is relived during the Easter Vigil through a journey along the path of biblical readings that retraces the main trajectory of salvation history. This is as if to suggest that God's power, culminating in Jesus' resurrection, even if it does not originate from history—because it comes from God, who is outside of history, and who creates it, even if it does not end up being part of history, because it has its culmination in God's mystery at the end of time—is realized as presence in history, thus as a commitment to history and to life, as the opening of history to its true, defined, and transcendent end. Therefore, the light of Christ, which is sung and that shines in the night of the Easter vigil, offers the opportunity to embrace the overall arc of human history to understand its deep meaning, as it is sung in the Easter Proclamation according to the Ambrosian rite, which states, "The unfolding of this holy Vigil embraces the entire mystery of our salvation; foretold events and prophecies of old come true in the rapid course of a single night."

Jesus' resurrection is therefore primarily a fact that belongs, in some way, to the history that is circumscribed in time and space; a historical event that is dated, witnessed, documented in its effects, and is at the same time an event of universal significance that concerns all of humanity; the event able to give every man and woman the full measure of his or her freedom. It is a historical event, an event of universal significance, better yet, of cosmic significance, the beginning of the global transformation of the world. It is an event of epochal significance because it transforms the sense of history while indicating its true direction; it shows that human history is on its way to becoming the great body of the risen humanity in the risen Christ. In Jesus' resurrection, which we proclaim on Easter day, we are certain that the God of life will not abandon us in the darkness of death and that God's divine life is at work within us already now, if we rely on God's extraordinary power.

A new original, inexhaustible source of life was infused into the world through the cosmic event of Christ's resurrection.

As Christians, we celebrate the event of Jesus' resurrection from the dead; an event that is realized and relived before the believers' eyes, in their hearts and in their lives on Easter Sunday. To understand the magnitude of this event of Jesus' resurrection, we must understand who Jesus Christ is, and to do so, we must look at him not only starting from here below, that is, from his humanity, but from above, as God the Father sees him, and who he actually is in God's plan and mystery. Seen from above, Jesus Christ is the origin of the universe, the one in view of whom all exists; the one for whom everything has being and life. Jesus' resurrection is therefore not a personal or private matter that concerns him only, but marks the passing of the universe to a new way of being; it is the revelation of what the whole universe truly is. The transitory universe has a renewed existence and recognizes its center in Jesus Christ and, with him and in him, in all the redeemed and in all the saved humanity.

We can therefore try to read Jesus' resurrection also from "above," that is, we can interpret Easter starting from God's plan. It then appears as the central event and what God wanted: the glory of the Son who became man, the Son glorified in his humanity; the Son's glorious reign with the Father, attracting to himself all humanity in his glory and in his life.

The Easter seen in this perspective, from "above," is the real one, the absolute one. The other one, the one seen through history, is like a piece or part of a larger picture. If we look at it as a part, we cannot understand it well; it appears to be a fact, albeit very relevant, among many others. Instead, Easter is the event around which everything else revolves. That is why the resurrection we celebrate is a historical event but of cosmic proportions; it is from this event that the global transfiguration of the world occurs; it is also the event that transforms the sense of human life; better yet, it indicates its true meaning and fulfills it.

This is the announcement that changed the world: "The Lord has risen indeed" (Luke 24:34). On the blessed Easter night, God raised the Son, breathing eternal life in his mortal flesh; breathing life in his body as at the beginning of Creation. Jesus is not risen like Lazarus because he rises again to attain a new and eternal life; his body is all bright and transparent, not limited by time and space. Jesus' resurrected body contains, as in a germ, all the transformed and renewed Creation in its original splendor; Jesus' glorious body incorporates within itself all of us. What we will be one day in eternity is already present, because we already are part of Jesus' immortal life. This is the most decisive event in the history of Creation: the Son of God has entered into death; to a certain extent he allowed himself to be defeated by it, but then he rose again so he could be with us always, weaving his presence with our existence, revealing himself to be the meaning of our life here on earth and of our daily events, regenerating our freedom.

Jesus' resurrection is a prelude to the final Parousia; and the earth rejoices, as it is illumined by such splendor.

Therefore, in celebrating Easter, not only do we remember a historical event, but we also grasp the enduring significance of this event; it is not just the memory of Jesus of Nazareth's death and his mysterious encounter with his disciples, but it is an event that changes history and gives a new meaning to the course of human events.

We can briefly sum up this new meaning by saying, first of all, that injustice is not the last word. Jesus was killed unjustly, but his resurrection reestablishes him; thus, injustice is washed away, as it were, and is exceeded in Jesus' resurrection.

Further, death itself is not the last word: Jesus did not end his noble career as reformer and Messiah on the cross, or in the tomb, because Jesus lives. As a result, from that moment, death is no longer the last word for the cycle of human existence. Moreover, if we reflect more deeply, we realize that in this event, the Father shows that he loves humanity immensely and proves it by sending his Son to die for humanity and restore, through his resurrection, life in every man and woman. Therefore, human history is no longer the exclusive pastime of men, always and variously in conflict with each other, or joining forces in different ways on earth; human history is no longer the history of a solitary humanity on one of the many possible worlds; God is with humanity, with its suffering, with its death; God the Father is with us, offering us his life.

"The Lord has risen indeed" means, therefore, that Jesus' resurrection makes true, gives being, gives body, and gives substance to the whole complex of things that, starting from the resurrection of Christ, form our reality, our reality of Christians and of being Church. "The Lord has risen indeed" means that the eternal life awaiting us is true, that Jesus' beatitudes are true, that poverty is true, that the expectation of God's kingdom is true, and that all those aspects that form the Christian moral world, the world of the Spirit, the world's search for God in the heart and in the depths of human decisions are true. It means that the cross, suffering, and death have a meaning, as do loyalty, purity, and our Easter vigil in church. It means that to pray, to forgive one's enemies, and to become neighbor to others makes sense. It means that to place the

Eucharist at the center of our lives makes sense and that all these realities are not fabricated, or false, or part of our everyday life, which we often consider to be the only true life; these realities *are* our true life; these are the real substance of things, our true reality. Everything else, all other daily experiences have value because they are founded on this reality, on this spiritual world of the risen Christ.

The reality of bodily existence that lies before us with its apparent physicality has its own unique sense of being ordered to this other reality, the reality of the risen Christ, and to all that is derived from that reality. The reality of the risen Christ is the only reality that matters; it is the one that gives meaning and joy to all our physical, bodily, human, well-being and to all our efforts; it also gives meaning to the mountains, the snow, the waterfalls, the stars, the automobiles, the main highways, the skyscrapers, the cathedrals. It all makes sense from the perspective of Jesus' true resurrection; everything assumes consistency, strength, internal logic, and value in relation to this supreme value that is the risen Christ, who is the culmination of Creation and of life that from him radiates to the world.

It is from this message of Jesus' resurrection, which we should spread worldwide, from this resurrection that already now, regardless of any historical utopia of the future, changes human history and allows humanity to turn the page, that the Church is born. From this missionary impulse, from the power of the Spirit to bear witness to the new life coming from Jesus' resurrection emerges the possibility of a true morality, of a genuine justice, of a life whose traits are not selfishness and exploitation but humble gift of self; from Jesus' resurrection emerges the possibility of striving for a lasting and true peace among humankind, starting from our hearts renewed by the remission of sins, restored in our conscience, reassured by the certainty of being God's children, nourished by the hope of everlasting life; and, all this, thanks to the grace and power of Jesus' resurrection.

Ultimately, Jesus is in God, God the Father is in him, Jesus is the Son of God, Jesus is God, therefore, Jesus is not on the margins of this world; God is not at the edge of the universe; God is the necessary horizon of all that we are and of everything we do, so that we always are in God. God is both the center and the heart of all realities because everything is in God and God is in everything. Therefore, the risen Jesus is the horizon, the center of all history, of all life, and of every single day.

Christ's resurrection reveals, therefore, the sense of all human history, the sense of all the events that we live every day; it does so through that word of hope that is proclaimed by Peter in his speech in the Acts of the Apostles: "But God raised him up, having freed him from death, because it was impossible for him to be held in its power" (2:24). Reading these words makes us wonder: Why was it not possible? Unfortunately, we are used to the fact, to the reality, that death is not only possible but even inevitable, and that everything is subject to its rule. When we think about death, we think with sadness to the inevitability of all that death is: sadness, hatred, wars, destruction. Peter proclaims, "Because it was impossible for him to be held in its [death's] power." The mystery of God in the risen Christ is therefore victory over death; victory over all that, in some way, belongs to death. It is the victory over everything in our lives and existence that conveys the meaning and the sadness of death. Christ's resurrection reveals the sense, the meaning, the direction of the entire human reality that strives toward life and, in each of us, to the fullness of expression of our freedom.

Christ's resurrection restores our freedom; heals its illusions; assigns to our freedom within history authentic and constructive goals; enables us to cooperate with the love of God, who gives life to all, in humble and industrious expectation of the resurrection of the whole human being and of the universe that has already begun with Christ's resurrection, but that will have its full realization and its glorious manifestation when and as the Father wills.

Our freedom, therefore, is also called to rise again, to participate in this fullness of Christ's life, to engage in history for life's sake. The restoration of our freedom finds in our baptism a concrete point of reference.

Christ is with us, in us, in baptism; he lives in us and walks with us in our lives; but he asks us to express ourselves clearly in history to transform and change it in favor of life, just as his resurrection changes the course of history from death to life. Christ asks us to do it courageously in the sense of both renunciation and courageous profession of faith: renunciation of everything in us that is an ally of death; everything in us that is power and aggression; everything that is hasty obsessiveness, selfishness, and desire to satisfy only and exclusively ourselves; everything that is disengagement, resignation, despair, and sadness. We are asked, committing ourselves at the moment of our baptism, to express a bold and firm profession of faith; a faith built and experienced around the figure of Christ who died and rose again; thus, a faith that is not only professed with words, or only expressed in the bottom of our hearts, but one that is also brought forth with our hands toward life, engaging ourselves in history and in daily problems, expressing ourselves in courageous decisions, taken through our freedom.

The path we undertake the evening of the celebration of the Easter Vigil is that of a long journey; a journey that could be primarily defined as the "path of memory": the path of the Church's memory and the path of Israel's memory over the course of the nine biblical readings that lead from Creation to the new humanity, in the person of the risen Jesus Christ. Over this course, we undertake another journey that could be called the "path of hope," or the "path of desires"; a path that is symbolized by the catechumens who traditionally on the Easter Vigil expect to receive baptism, symbolized by the signs we use during the celebration of Mass: fire, light, and water.

While the path of memory takes us back to the past, the path of hope allows us to look to the future: it is the path of Christian freedom, the path of a renewed life, and a new way of living. Therefore, it is not only about eternal life, the life expecting us after death, but of a new life, a different life that is already manifest and almost bursts out from the old situations of this earthly existence of ours. At this point, it is important to understand what relationship is fulfilled in the risen Christ between the path of the past (the path of memory) and the path of hope (the path of the future). What is the relationship between tradition and freedom? And translating these things into our human frailty, what is the relationship between our regrets and reminiscences of the past and our illusions, or delusions, of the future? What relationship is fulfilled in the risen Christ between all that is behind us, in our history, in the history of the Church and of the world and all that is before us, in the future of our lives, in the future of the Church, and the future of humanity?

To this question, we can synthetically propose an answer that is suggested by the celebration of the Easter Vigil: the risen Jesus Christ does not undo the past of Israel, but resurrects its memory, creating, in his glorious body, the unity between the past and the future, between memory and desire, between tradition and freedom; creating the unity of the new humanity who lives in itself, without contradictions, the memories of the past and the hopes of the future, the link with tradition, and the creative freedom that lies ahead.

The Easter Vigil, therefore, offers and realizes a remarkable connection between past and future, between memory and hope, between tradition and freedom. Perhaps we can find strange, looking at ourselves, the fact that the hope and freedom of humanity's future is closely linked to the memory and the recollection of the past. But what is our idea of the future, of freedom, and of hope? Perhaps sometimes we are tempted to think, like many people of our time, that the future is an absolute beginning, something that originates exclusively from ourselves as a self-sufficient unfolding of projects and involvements in the world and society. Then we think of our freedom as an autonomous beginning that has to be projected on external objects, events, and realities to transform them in one's own image. In this case, the past is seen simply as a distant time, something gone and to be forgotten, full of regrets and sadness, or at the most, as an accumulation of experiences that form the backdrop to the achievements of today and tomorrow. This is why modern men and women like to present themselves as without memory, without a past, without predecessors, thus protesting, in principle, every tradition that seems to constrain their freedom.

But if we look more deeply into ourselves, we find that there are actually in us different and opposite feelings, thoughts, and emotions; along with stirrings of self-sufficiency and self-assertion, there is also in us and in the world around us deep love for parents, gratitude for friends, awe for a mystery greater than us. If we open ourselves, even if only as human beings, to understand these things, then we feel that our freedom cannot be understood as an absolute beginning.

2. A SHOUT OF JOY, A CRY OF VICTORY

Easter is not like any other celebration; or a feast a bit more solemn than others, as sometimes we read or hear from the comments of the media ("One of the most solemn feasts"), but it is *the* feast in which all the other feasts find their source, and without which the others would be meaningless. "Christ has been raised from the dead and has given life to all": these are the words of the entrance song of the most solemn celebration of Easter. They proclaim the risen Lord, and Jesus' resurrection is the condition on which the Christian faith either stands or falls. For this reason, the Easter Proclamation invites us to rejoice, saying: "Joy to the Church, radiating with living splendor, and may this temple resound with the cheers of the celebrating people."

Similarly, it is worth remembering that the beautiful antiphon to Mary "Regina Coeli Laetare. Alleluia"

(Queen of Heaven, rejoice. Alleluia), which is sung especially during the forty days of the Easter season, reveal very well Our Lady's joy for her Son's resurrection, and with her, and in her, the joy of the Church, which is our joy. Although the Gospels do not make any mention of a visit of Mary to the tomb, nor of an apparition of Jesus to her, Mary, Jesus' Mother, is certainly the first person present in the mystery of the resurrection, the first participant in the consolation given by Jesus to the Father. She who from the very beginning fully accepted the Word of God; she who believed and carried in her womb the Word; she who received in her arms for the last time her dead Son, is the first dawn of the morning after Saturday and wants us to live fully the grace of the blessed night of the vigil and the boundless horizon of hope that this grace communicates.

Therefore, the cry of the Church, the cry of joy and victory, passed down from generation to generation, from the beginning of Christianity to us today is this: "The Lord has risen indeed." It is useful to first reflect on a word, that adverb, "has risen *indeed*," which is the triumphant expression with which the eleven apostles in the Upper Room welcomed the two disciples of Emmaus who had come to them to tell how they had seen Jesus along the way, and he was made known to them in the breaking of the bread. The eleven respond, "The Lord has risen *indeed*, and he has appeared to Simon!" (Luke 24:34). This word, *indeed*, is not to be interpreted as a simple way to indicate the cry of victory. In its original form, it refers to something deeper, as it recalls an ontological reality that touches the being of the world, of humanity, and history with its many paths. The Greek root word that we render with "indeed" (i.e., οντως) means "in the reality of being, at the heart of being."

If we try to ask what awareness we, as Church, have when we launch this cry: "The Lord has risen indeed," we can identify a triple awareness of the Church and of Christians in relation to the realities of God and Jesus. There may in fact be a false, a weak, and a genuine awareness.

The false awareness is that of those who hear the words "Christ has risen indeed; this is the center of life; what gives value to everything else"; but they consider them only words, literature, religious themes, folklore, culture, and so on. When there is only this reaction to these words, perhaps they think to be part of the Church because they physically go to church sometimes, but do not participate effectively in the life of the Church; they are not really Christians, and the joy of Easter then remains an enigma, or a mere formality linked to a certain time and season.

Instead, there is a real awareness, but still weak, and perhaps pertaining to many, because it was also the awareness of the apostles at the beginning which made it hard for them to believe, that of Thomas, for example, or that of the disciples of Emmaus, who needed time to understand. It is the awareness of those who repeat this cry: "Christ has risen indeed," but repeat it without engaging their intellect; they would like to, but then they feel a little distant, neither in nor out. They say to themselves, "Yes, there must be a world of the Spirit, an eternal life, there has to be a meaning to prayer. I also try to do something similar; yet, it just does not sink in; I do not surrender to it as children in the arms of their mothers; I have mental reservations, both conscious and unconscious. I'd rather be a bit with a foot in both camps, a bit in the reality of material things that attract me, and a bit in the reality of Jesus. I would not dare risk my life on Jesus' Word." This means that this awareness, the sense of being children of God, and the felt certainty of the risen One is still weak. Hence, in this case, our prayer must be like the prayer that brings us back to the

Gospel: "I believe [Lord]; help my unbelief!" (Mark 9:24), that is to say, Lord, you know everything; you know that I would like to love you and believe; increase my faith.

Finally, there is the genuine awareness of those who launch this cry and entrust their lives to it. It is the awareness with which Mary, Jesus' Mother, believed, as did the women at the tomb, the saints of all time, from St. Augustine to St. Ambrose, and St. Charles Borromeo to all the holy and true Christians of today. It is that awareness that stirs and rouses within us the joy of Easter, the certainty of the presence of the Spirit in us.

This faith is not born in us by an act or an effort of the imagination. It does not even originate from a rigorous historical study, even if science can lead to the realization that the testimony of the first apostles to Jesus' resurrection is worthy of belief; but this is nothing but the premise of an act that we perform with our whole selves and that is aroused in us by the grace of the Holy Spirit, which inclines us to adhere with love to that truth, to the cry of the resurrection that pervades the universe and gives a new meaning to all things. It is the Spirit of God that arouses in us that sincere cry: "Christ has risen indeed"; it is the Spirit of God that makes us say with full truthfulness, "Father";

Christ Is Risen from the Dead 69

it is the Spirit that predisposes us to read the meaning of our life events in the light of the resurrection.

We must therefore ask the Lord to grant us to welcome him with the same joy with which the women at the tomb welcomed the cry of life; with the same joy with which this cry was welcomed by his Mother, the Virgin Mary.

Like Mary Magdalene and the other women are told: "Go and tell my brothers" (Matt 28:10), so each one of us, called by Jesus brother or sister, feels within oneself the joy of proclaiming to all others that we are brothers and sisters, that our every gesture of love creates eternity in our midst, that death does not frighten us anymore because life already reigns in every loving, genuine, and truthful gesture.

This is the true Easter announcement: I have seen the Lord; I have had experience of him; now I know that we live in him; now I know that eternity is already here; now I know that nothing else can make me despair of the future because the future has entered my life. The Lord has come into us.

This cry, this announcement: "I have seen the Lord" (John 20:18) and that he called us all brothers and sisters is the announcement from which stems the missionary nature of the Church—not a proselytizing intended to augment herself or her own glory, but a joyful irradiation, a free and disinterested irradiation of this joy received in one's heart. Now I know that death cannot harm me anymore; that no worry, fear, or subjugation of this world and everyday reality can oppress me because there is within me the source of eternity and freedom that is the risen Jesus Christ.

The cry of the resurrection is the angel's reassurance to the women at the tomb that the risen Jesus is going before them into Galilee. Even these women, therefore, do not see Jesus, but are comforted by a word of faith and hope. The cry "Jesus has risen" thus consists of two aspects: it is the cry of faith because it announces what has already happened for good in Christ, and the cry of hope because it announces what will be when we will rise and we will see him resurrected in the fullness of his glory. This cry is like a synthesis of all the events of this great mystery of salvation that are recalled in the different readings of the Easter Vigil, and it is also the cry corresponding to that of the Crucified on whom we fix our attention on Good Friday: "My God, my God, why have you forsaken me?" (Matt 27:46). On Good Friday, we reflect on how this cry summarizes all human despair, all the darkness, the cruelty of which we hear about every day, and all these nights of human civilization. This cry, "My God, my God, why have you forsaken me?" sums up all the despair and the cruelty and embraces it all in a love that, as the Evangelist John says, loves "to the end" (13:1). The cry of the resurrection, "The Lord has risen indeed" (Luke 24:34), is the divine response to Jesus' cry of pain: "Why have you forsaken me?"

On the night when the guards kept watch at Jesus' sealed tomb, when the Sanhedrin kept vigilant lest the tomb should be opened, again the Lord passed over, thus responding to the cry of the Son: "Why have you forsaken me?" The Lord passes over and there emerges the great cry of Jesus' resurrection; and the priest also, by the grace of his ministry, the evening of Easter gives this announcement three times and in different directions, so the whole world can hear this cry: "Christ, who was crucified, has been raised" (see Mark 16:6).

The certainty, therefore, of this cry of joy, which corresponds to Jesus' cry of distress on the cross, is the certainty proclaiming that every abyss of evil in this world has already been engulfed by an abyss of good; each death finds its counterweight of life that prevails over every burden of disease and death; every crisis finds its solution; every sadness finds its timely and overwhelming joy; every despair finds its glorious resurrection. This certainty and confidence have been proclaimed at our baptism, when they were bestowed through faith and the gift of the virtue of hope.

Thus, God loves us; Jesus is alive in our midst. Jesus comes to us with his forgiveness and his salvation. Jesus has risen for us. The resurrection is the participation of Jesus' human body in the glory of the Son of God and anticipates what will happen to all of us who believe. The overwhelming power of Jesus' resurrection enters into us, in fact, first of all through the sacramental signs (baptism, confirmation, Eucharist). First, through the sign of baptism: all baptized can repeat with the community of the Church those words that are already part of the Jewish Passover liturgy: "God brought me from slavery to freedom, from sadness to joy, from mourning to celebration, from darkness to light, from confusion to redemption. So in God's presence I say: Alleluia." The Alleluia, which is sung after the proclamation of the risen One, is placed on the lips of our brothers and sisters through the sacrament of baptism.

On the night of Easter, after the sacrament of baptism, the catechumens receive confirmation, which is the perfect gift of the Holy Spirit. Then, all together we approach the Eucharist, knowing that every time we communicate to Jesus' eucharistic body, he conforms us ever more fully to his condition as Son of the Father who is in heaven.

As a result of the night of the Easter Vigil, all Christians await the gift of the risen Christ that we receive initially in baptism, then in confirmation, and always in the Eucharist, which is the Holy Spirit. As Pope John Paul II also said in his encyclical on the Holy Spirit, *Dominum et Vivificantem*: "Through the gift of grace, which comes from the Holy Spirit, man enters a 'new life,' is brought into the supernatural reality of the divine life itself and becomes a 'dwelling-place of the Holy Spirit,' a living temple of God. For through the Holy Spirit, the Father and the Son come to him and take up their abode with him. In the communion of grace with the Trinity, man's 'living area' is broadened and raised up to the supernatural level of divine life."

The main announcement, the announcement that makes present the event of Jesus' resurrection, "Christ has risen indeed," is repeated three times in the liturgy, just as in the Scriptures all that has an absolute certainty are repeated three times and that is the foundation of many others realities. This is, in synthesis, the kerygma, that is, the proclamation of salvation, whose characteristics are simplicity, clarity, immediacy, and the power of its proclamation.

The impact force of the kerygma, of the fundamental Easter proclamation, however is combined with the daily patience of the Christian practice, of the configuration of a maturity of faith that is efficacious when it becomes a testimony that is daily, humble, persuasive, and steadfast in love. Certainly, nowadays many feel the need of a strong Christian commitment—and rightly so; we want a proclamation that is bold, unmistakable; a proclamation that reaches the consciences and offers to everyone the certainty of Jesus' resurrection, the revelation of the mystery of God. In order to be so, this certainty must be combined with the daily patience of community building; it must not be prone to anger nor in opposition to contemporary society as such, but rather regard it with patience, as humanity awaiting salvation. It must strongly reaffirm faith in the risen One; it must restore the Christian announcement to its original force. But this assertive and authoritative announcement, "Christ has risen indeed," must then become attentive to history and to the complexity of human affairs.

Yes, it is true, we need to restore strength to the Christian announcement and this strength should be directed toward the rediscovery of the announcement through the power of the Spirit, of Jesus' death and resurrection, and of God's authority in history. However, often we cannot get the real sense of the liberation to which Jesus' resurrection leads; we cultivate the imaginative and illusory idea that everything can and must change immediately; that, starting from today, there should be no more diseases, pain, or social unrest, injustice, and war. When the sun sets on a day of celebration like that of Easter Sunday, the following Monday, or Tuesday, we resume our week and we realize that people continue to suffer and die, then we are disappointed; we expected friendliness and peace, or perhaps that the superpowers' negotiations during Holy Week would have led to disarmament; instead nothing has changed.

Then, we easily fall into disappointment, and we think that tomorrow and the day after weapons will still be produced, and killing and violence will resume. So, what does the paschal victory of Christ mean? How can we make room within us for Christ's paschal joy? Christ's paschal victory that we celebrate certainly has to do with all the evil in the world, and therefore sin, war, violence, and weapons; yet, it all starts from us. There is certainly also the time and the condition for the final victory, and this is already present and unmistakable in

Jesus' resurrection: the Lord is preparing this final victory of the Son for human history, but we do not know neither the time nor the moment.

However, one thing is certain right now: that this victory takes place primarily in us, in me; it takes place in those who proclaim Jesus' resurrection and, through me, it takes place in the community, in cities, and thus in society at large. We are the firstfruit of the risen Christ; we are his revelation. If our freedom is able to gather its most beautiful energies to rely on Christ and make room for his love, then we truly become the beginning of a new world, starting with ourselves, as we are loved, forgiven, and renewed by Jesus' living presence.

Our current culture, with the enormous and urgent tasks that it offers us in the material and social world, at times runs the risk of making us forget this primacy of the person. Jesus' resurrection, by presenting humanity as the first work of the new creation, the new man, the risen Christ, and by presenting the woman, Mary Magdalene, whose dried out tears are the firstfruit of a conscience restored to truth and joy, invites us to an authentic humanism, to the primacy of being over having and doing.

Finally, it is important that we all ask ourselves what the joy of Easter is for us, its meaning, what it says to us, and what it contains. Does not this joy that we aspire to run the risk perhaps of being something superficial that we say with our lips, and that deep down we would like to be true to the end, but don't know how? Or, in the best-case scenario, if we look with faith to the true source of this Easter joy that is the risen Christ, do we not run perhaps here into another risk: to express a joy that we could define as "a joy made of forgetfulness" and founded on oblivion? In other words, a joy that is simply based on the fact that Christ is now alive, that we affirm in faith, receive in faith, proclaim in faith, but almost forget Jesus' death and passion, his cross, the nails, and the scourges. It is a little like believing that all these things never happened; as if everything related to Jesus' passion and death was only a bad dream. But Jesus' passion and death were not a bad dream; they were real, and they are still real here today, among us, in the suffering of so many.

Thus, we can also be surprised that the hope of Easter joy does not take away the suffering of the world; we can be surprised that after a brief euphoria, we end the day after Easter facing the usual problems: diseases, injustice, violence, hunger. How, then, are we to understand the joy of Easter without turning it into a superficial, or artificial, joy? A joy that is not just based on forgetfulness, or on the omission of Christ's sufferings and our own? A joy, therefore, that does not last for just a short moment, but one that marks, like Christ's resurrection, a change in life?

The biblical readings of the Easter Mass help to answer these questions. The biblical readings of the liturgy fill those who listen carefully with a significant reminder of Christ's past, that is, they are a source of memory, or we could say of historical realism, which gives depth and texture to the joy of Jesus' resurrection. As mentioned earlier, we are often tempted by a superficial, almost forgetful, joy; a joy that sees in Jesus' resurrection simply a happy reason to forget the painful events of Jesus' human and mortal history, and act as if they had never happened, as if they never had to be in the first place. Instead, the Word of God says that Jesus is the risen One who suffered and died. Better yet, Jesus had to die.

Luke's Gospel goes as far as to say, reporting Jesus' words to the disciples of Emmaus, that "the Messiah should suffer these things" (24:26).

Thus, we understand why the Word of God reveals that the Lord's new life is not simply the annulment of his death on the cross, as if it had never been, like something to forget, like when we remove the crucifix from our altars, our churches, from our homes, from the places where it is still honored. The Lord's new life is not the annulment of Jesus' death on the cross, but it is the revelation, the unveiling of the prodigious vitality that was already present in Jesus' life and death. In Jesus' death, experienced in abandonment to the Father, as well as in love and dedication to others, there was already the secret of his life, which he had surrendered with love for his own in the sacrament of the Eucharist, the Eucharist of the Last Supper, declaring to freely give up his life out of love for all of us in abandonment to the Father.

Therefore, the liturgical readings recall this realism, this continuity among Jesus' death, his suffering, and his life. The Acts of the Apostles, for example, speak of what Jesus did and taught from the very beginning until the day he was taken up into heaven. All that Jesus accomplished from the very beginning was under the sign of love, thus revealing life.

In the same reading, Jesus warns the disciples from fantasizing about immediately reconstituting the kingdom of God in Israel, inviting them instead to be his witnesses to the whole world. Even the apostles wanted to forget everything and immediately embrace a new way of being that would eliminate all suffering and responsibility, but the risen Christ says to them, "No, this is the time to go and testify in this world and in this historical moment my life as the risen One."

Even the ancient profession of faith that St. Paul recalls in his First Letter to the Corinthians, which transmits one of the oldest confessions of faith, the creed of the early Christians, of the first disciples, of those who had seen Jesus alive after his death, of those who had touched his wounds and recognized in him the Crucified, the One now risen; even this creed says that the risen Jesus is the Jesus who died for our sins and was buried.

In John's Gospel, which seems almost to recount an episode that is unique and private as it involved only one person, Mary Magdalene, the revelation of the risen Christ to her occurs by the pronouncing of her name, Mary. This woman felt called, felt recognized, and in turn recognized the Lord; in recognizing him, she remembers all the events of Jesus' life until his death; she also recalls the intensity of the gift with which Jesus loved the Father, spoke of God's love, and expressed this love until death.

Therefore, the Word of God at Easter invites us to deepen the relationship between the two essential paschal moments, that is, Jesus' death and his resurrection.

The latter, Jesus' resurrection, exceeds the first not in the sense of abolishing it, but in the sense of the full development of life already present in Jesus' death out of love for us. The light of the resurrection does not obscure the cross, but helps the believer to understand the mystery of life and love emanating from it. If we neglect this connection, which is the intimate structure of the paschal mystery, that is, Jesus' passion, death, and resurrection, then we are exposed to disappointments, at times even profound ones. The joy and wish of Easter, in fact, must consider reality; a reality that, from both the external point of view of history and from the closer one of the course of events that in their materiality surround us, apparently, has not changed at all.

Around us, sickness, death, hatred, social unrest continue to exist. Therefore Easter does not take away these things immediately, but it confirms that if Christ is alive in the glory of God, in the fullness of God's love; if Christ is alive in the Church and in history; and if Christ is alive in us, then all these realities not only do not prevent us from loving, but in them, we can hope and love more and more. For those who have understood something of life and love, this is a word that says it all: Christ assures us that those who live in love, even in these realities of suffering and death, are not abandoned by God but are welcomed, loved, and initiated into the fullness of life and joy. Who loves receives life; who loves receives the life of Christ in oneself and is made capable of giving life, of transmitting life to others.

Therefore, this is the true joy of Easter; a joy that is not superficial and forgetful, nor one that is false, or lasts only for a moment; but a joy capable of retaining a profound memory of the cross of Christ; and a joy that helps us to find the paths along which we can announce the true hope of Easter to our brothers and sisters.

3. THE CHRISTIAN RESPONSE TO DEATH

A prayer of praise of the Easter liturgy says, "Your Son, with a death truly blessed, conquers forever our death." This is the main point of the Feast of Easter: in Jesus' death, our death, even though it retains its biological reality, is neither a dark conclusion nor a desperate dissolution, nor an emergency exit to nothingness. It is a conquered reality, that is, it has been tamed in its fierceness so it no longer dominates human thoughts and expectations.

But perhaps someone might think, even on Easter night, what sense does it make to celebrate the Lord's resurrection, when our world continues to be marked by suffering, by banality, by hatred, by hostilities, and by wars? What sense does it make to rejoice for Christ's victory over death when death still exists and is the only certainty we have about the future?

This is perhaps the most poignant question that may arise during the holy night of Easter; the one that emerges within us while to the world we say, "Christ has risen." But if he has risen, why do we still have to die? Why do we experience still so many crimes, so many tragedies, so many tears? Well, it is precisely for this reason that on the evening of Holy Saturday, we go to church to celebrate Easter because Jesus' Easter does not automatically take us into the realm of dreams, but reaches us deep in our hearts to let us undertake, with joy and hope, that journey of purification and sincerity, and validation of our lives, which has as its goal the certainty of a life that will never end. Once we have left the church, Easter does not give us back to an unreal world, but to our authentic existence, a life of faith, hope, and love. If we understand this, Easter is within us and begins to work around us.

With all the elaborate and quite long ceremonies that are celebrated during the Easter Triduum, the Church wants to effectively communicate one thing:

she's happy for Jesus' resurrection and that we also are happy because we feel that in Jesus' resurrection there is something new and beautiful for us and not just for him.

We are happy for Jesus after having contemplated him hanging from the cross, pierced and crucified; after contemplating Mary weeping at the foot of the cross, and pierced herself by the sword of sorrow. We are glad that all this is over, and over for good; but we are happy for us too, because we sense, if only vaguely, that in our case, there is no more the great fear of death and all its signs: sadness, anxiety, illness, hurry, distress, all that which threatens to engulf our lives. Thanks to Jesus' resurrection all these things have lost their poison: true, we can still be a little frightened, and death can still sting; but it is like a poisonous snake left with no poison, which cannot do much harm or cause that tragic distress that without the Lord's resurrection there always was between us and death and all its signs and effects, throwing humanity into despair and hopelessness. We feel that all this is over; we sense that the following words from John's Book of Revelation are already beginning to come true: "Death will be no more; mourning and crying and pain will be no more, for the first things have passed away" (21:4).

Easter is our most glorious feast, the ultimate Christian feast, the feast of the Church, the feast of life, the feast of victory over death. The Gospel recounts that Mary Magdalene was at the tomb, "weeping." This verb is repeated four times: "But Mary stood weeping outside the tomb"; "As she wept, she bent over to look into the tomb"; "[The angels] said to her, 'Woman, why are you weeping?'"; "Jesus said to her, 'Woman, why are you weeping? Whom are you looking for?'" (see John 20:11–15). What does Mary's weeping signify? It encapsulates every cry of humanity in the face of death; it embodies the confusion, the loss, the pain, the inner turmoil that humanity feels facing the victory of death over life, of evil over good, of darkness over light, of injustice over justice, of deceit over truth.

The cry of Mary Magdalene is a legitimate, heart-rending, and hopeless cry because for her, the tomb represented the end of her friend's life. She stared at it almost obsessively, as if it was the last thing that one can look at; something now closed, concluded, definitive; something that leaves no room for the novelty of God.

As long as we mourn with her and we remain in sadness, we do not see anything but the tomb; we cannot even recognize the risen Christ who is next to us.

This is our human condition: humanity meets its own death, unlike animals who sense death approaching only when they are threatened or when it is imminent; we instead are always aware that our life ends with death. This thought weighs on us throughout our life: to be familiar with death is for us already part of our dying. We exist as always and inevitably in relation to our end. We read our life as a set of already determined moments that has an irrevocable end: contemporary philosophers have spoken of "being-for-death."

Of course we can, as we often do, remove this thought; we can tell ourselves that it is not worth thinking about, and this is also a way to take a stand in the face of death. Therefore, we cannot but take a position of some kind in front of the certainty of our biological and physical end. Our position is either one of acceptance or desperation, or more often, we refuse to think about it, we remove it. However, we cannot but wonder what will happen to us after death; what will become of all those riches that, after all, have been the true meaning of our lives, that is, love, loyalty, pain, friendship, responsibility, freedom, conscience, service.

We feel that these things cannot simply be treated as molecules that are transformed to give rise to a new biological cycle; these things are different in nature.

The Christian response that we receive at Easter confirms our hunch: the Christian response does not simply tell us that these things will last, thus, that we too one day, even after death, will continue to live, and there will be for us an eternity. The Christian response that Jesus' resurrection gives us is that eternity is already here; the new and definitive life has already entered here, now, in my experience. It arises already here and now from my abandonment to Jesus, who died and rose again, from my faith, modeled after that of Jesus in the Father. Thus, the eternity of Jesus who has conquered death already enters in me and is part of my experience from this very moment: the thought of physical death is not removed, but is sublimated and transfigured by the certainty that eternity is already here and now, as part of my experience, and that I am in the eternity of Jesus, in the glorious and ultimate life of Jesus, that he is in me and I am with the Father who lives and will always live.

I experience this everytime I make an act of faith or love, everytime I receive the Eucharist, or another sacrament. This experience of eternity is implied by the grace of the risen One in every truly free moral act, in every act we perform not for reason of pure convenience but because it is right and true, because it must be done precisely that way, even if that way means against our own interests. Every time that each one of us acts this way in our lives, we participate in the gift that God makes of his eternity, of God's being always true, just, unconditionally good; of God's revelation to us in truth, fidelity, love, and righteousness of Jesus.

The joy of Easter consists in letting ourselves be seized by this transforming power of the Spirit of the risen One who opens our eyes and makes us recognize that the tomb is no longer frightening because it is empty; that the world has opened itself to the life of God within us; and that in our hearts there is already a space of eternity that is created in the most simple aspects of everyday life because everybody is invited to be part of this eternity of Jesus that shines today in the Church and in the life of each one of us.

To speak of joy this way does not mean to ignore the pain, suffering, and death that is so much a part of our life here on earth, but it means to discover its meaning in the cross. It is the joy of being a new creature, of living the certainty of the proximity and the presence of the risen Christ, the joy of being able to understand history from the inside and from a higher perspective, the joy to evaluate things and people according to their definitive dimension, the joy of feeling that the final encounter with Jesus is at hand.

John Paul II's words come to mind; in particular, those in *Evangelium Vitae*, which can well be defined as a "paschal" encyclical because it announces the Easter gift par excellence, that is, the gift of eternal life. John Paul II wrote, "In Christ, the Gospel of life is definitively proclaimed and fully given. This is the Gospel which, already present in the Revelation of the Old Testament, and indeed written in the heart of every man and woman, has echoed in every conscience 'from the beginning,' from the time of creation itself." Then he continued by stating, "In Jesus, the 'Word of life,' God's eternal life is thus proclaimed and given." In effect, during the Easter vigil, we proclaim this life and we do so in the context of the entire human history that resonates throughout the liturgy; we do so in the context of peace and war, of love and hatred, of light and darkness. With his resurrection, Jesus has opened for us the kingdom of the Father, the kingdom of peace, love, and light: a kingdom that grows in us even though we can feel it almost imperceptibly, but it does grow in us because everything in the world and in history is drawn to the risen One; everything is drawn to the Crucified, lifted up from the earth, and restored to life by the Father.

What we call "Jesus' resurrection" assures us that everything has changed in the innermost aspect of every reality. Already in the depth of every transient reality, sin and death have been conquered, and the seed of eternity is already in all our daily actions. Jesus is waiting for all creatures who yearn for the glorification of their bodies: the risen Christ is in our lives, in our tears, in every death, as the secret joy of a life that is victorious even when it seems to be dying.

The resurrected Christ is in our suffering brothers and sisters to whom we become neighbors. In fact, as a great contemporary theologian said, "Man has value to the extent to which his face is illuminated by the ray of the divine face of the risen One, since, even while evolving and acting in history, he already breathes eternity." The risen Christ is in our helplessness as the power that can afford to appear weak because he is invincible. He is even in the midst of sin as the mercy of eternal life ready to wait until the end. Jesus is the heart of this earthly reality, the secret seal of its eternal worth, and he tells us that for that very reason, we exist and we have to love even this earth that frightens and torments us.

4. CALLED BY NAME

The Gospel passage from St. John that we hear on Easter Sunday recounts Mary Magdalene's astonishing meeting with the risen Lord. At first, Mary Magdalene is unable to recognize him, then suddenly a great light dawns on her when she hears her name called out; she is caught by surprise, enthusiasm, and tenderness.

A very similar dynamic is found in the moment of St. Augustine's recognition and conversion. Just as the moment when Mary Magdalene hears her name called by Jesus: "Mary!" so it is with his baptism: "Augustine." This is how he describes, shortly after his conversion, his enthusiasm for the divine voice that called him; in his elaborate rhetoric, and to explain how he was called, Augustine uses a series of images that relate to all five senses of the body that were shaken by this call: "You called, shouted, broke through my deafness; you flared, blazed, banished my blindness; you lavished your fragrance, I gasped, and now I pant for you; I tasted you, and I hunger and thirst; you touched me, and I burned for your peace."

Mary Magdalene's search for the risen Christ at the tomb, without clearly knowing what she was looking for, still denotes an inner strength, a hope, a yearning, and a cry to the risen Christ. Jesus' word *Mary*, his calling her by name, represents a certain and divine response to a confused and uncertain search. But this confused and uncertain search is precious because it is the unavoidable experience of every human being when it comes to a minimum of authenticity and honesty with oneself and with one's life. Jesus' word to Mary is therefore very significant, as is Mary's search, in which we can see reflected all our searches for something that is beyond life, beyond the experiences of this life.

"Whom are you looking for?" (John 20:15). This question is very significant within the context of John's Gospel because these are the first words that Jesus spoke since he started his public ministry, as recounted in John's Gospel. To two disciples of John the Baptist who approached Jesus—who was still unknown to all—and wanted to know who he was, Jesus asked the question that contains his first historical words cited by the Evangelist: "What are you looking for?" (John 1:38). And at the end of the whole Gospel, Jesus' question returns in a more personal way: "Who are you looking for?" which is equivalent to saying, "You are looking for someone."

This is the meaning of the question that the risen Christ addresses to all: "You are looking for someone who can dry your tears away, someone who can love you with a faithful love, who can love you forever, who can save you. You do not know who you are looking for, but you are looking for your God." When Jesus' Word and Spirit ask us this question, then it resonates powerfully within us, and we feel in us the power of the risen Christ. It is our Passover experienced by each one of us when we open the tomb of our hearts to the power of the living Lord. If we listen to this question, if we try to answer it, then we will also hear like Mary Magdalene being called by name; we will feel personally called. "Jesus said to her, 'Mary!'" (John 20:16).

Thus, to Jesus' questions: "Woman, why are you weeping? Whom are you looking for?" (John 20:15), there are Mary Magdalene's answers. "Why are you weeping?" Because I fear death, because I feel crushed at the thought of the death of the one I love. "Whom are you looking for?" I am looking for life, for the resurrection of those whom I love, my own resurrection so that we can all love one another forever, the resurrection of Jesus whom I love. The answer to her questions is a simple calling her by name. Jesus said to her, "Mary!" Thus, no reasoning, no demonstration, but just a name called out with love; this voice makes us recognize the mystery. After hearing Jesus' voice, Mary

Magdalene turns completely toward him, no longer thinking of the tomb, no longer thinking of her past.

We are all freed from our past, from oppression, from neuroses, and our inability to express ourselves when we say to Jesus, "I am looking for you, I am looking for your resurrection," and feel called by name in baptism, confirmation, the Eucharist, in prayer during Easter time. We recognize that Jesus calls us to the fullness of life, and we say to him, just like Mary Magdalene, "Rabbouni! (which means Teacher)" (John 20:16); my Lord, my teacher, my teacher of life, you who give me everything, you are the Church's Lord, you who will never abandon us, you who put eternity, already now, on the path of my life and that of the Church.

Mary Magdalene recognizes Jesus only after Jesus called her by name, that is, Jesus reawakened her person; he regenerated her freedom and renewed in it the creative power with which God calls every human existence and assigns to each a mission in life. For this reason, we must let ourselves be called by the risen Christ; we must let him ask us why we are weeping today, what are our deepest sufferings, and not only try to forget them for a day or two. But we must allow him to go deeper and ask why we cry and what are our true sufferings. Then let us ask ourselves what and whom are we looking for, and even then let us dig deeper to see what is the subject of our search without limits. Then, we will realize that we seek a person, we seek him who rose for us. Asking ourselves wholeheartedly these same questions of this Gospel passage ("Why are you weeping? Whom are you looking for?") means to roll the stone from the tomb of our lives; it means to recognize Jesus alive, now and forever.

Mary Magdalene saw with her own eyes the One whom she no longer believed to see again; she heard a penetrating voice that she would have never thought to hear, and felt called by name: "Mary!" It is significant that Jesus revealed himself to her not by announcing the event that refers to him ("I have risen, I am alive"), but by pronouncing her name: "Mary!" It is, therefore, a personal revelation, an existential one that instills in this woman not only the certainty that Christ is alive, but the awareness of being known by him truly and deeply in her fullness and her dignity. This is how Jesus wants to meet us: he approaches each one of us today; he puts back on the right track our uncertain, con- fused, clumsy searches; he reveals to us that he loves us and calls us by name. Each one of us, therefore, can have the experience of the risen One, can discern the signs even if there is little hope in our hearts, even if tears roll down our cheeks.

5. WE DO NOT UNDERSTAND, BUT WE WILL

The passage from John's Gospel that is read on Easter Sunday describes in detail a meeting: that of Mary Magdalene with the risen Lord. Mary Magdalene came to the tomb early, saw with surprise the empty tomb, and ran to call Peter and John; they in turn ran to the tomb, saw that Jesus' body was not there, and returned to communicate the news to the other disciples. But it was Mary, however, who remained alone at the tomb weeping, because she thought that her friend and teacher was forever dead and just wanted to know where they had put his body. Mary represents here humanity always looking for a savior, but with inhibited and limited hope. Mary's search for Jesus was still very human; she looked for Jesus where he was not. Often we ourselves look for God where he is not: in patterns of human effectiveness, success, power, and easy satisfaction. But Jesus was not irritated by this mistaken and imperfect search on the part of Mary because he knew that there was much love in it and a deep yearning.

Therefore, what is the meaning of Mary Magdalene at the tomb looking for Jesus? It is the image of all our current, imperfect, and confused searches; it is something that is beyond this life and its narrow perspectives. If we understand this, then we see that the message of the resurrection is not just something that reaches us from the outside, like a beautiful story that in the end is quite obscure, unverifiable, and out of our reach.

This episode touches on a hope, an expectation, a yearning for the resurrection that is unconsciously in each of us, always. In each one of us there is a longing to hear that our dead loved ones were not dead at all, but rather alive and with us. This yearning is present not only when we have the very human fear of our own death because we are never truly and completely resigned to the idea of returning to nothing; because, as already stated by St. Paul and reaffirmed by St. Augustine, we do not want to die, even when we want to live with Christ. Even the martyr St. Cyprian stated, "We leave this life, not willingly, but because we are obliged and forced to."

It could also happen to us to feel, during the solemn proclamation of the Lord's Passover, in that same embarrassing and disorienting situation in which the first apostles, Jesus' contemporaries, and witnesses of his resurrection, found themselves.

That unique situation is remembered in more than one page of the readings traditionally associated with the Easter season. In these authentic documents of the first Christian communities, we do not come across an easy enthusiasm in the proclamation of the risen One, but a certain slowness to believe, a certain caution and distrust, and difficulty to adapt to the new reality of things. It is as if fresh air were entering a room closed for too long, like a new world coming into an old world that finds it hard to accept, like the new wine that breaks the old wineskins. This situation is particularly evident in Mary Magdalene as mentioned in John's Gospel: Mary wept and failed to recognize that the one who was standing in front of her was precisely Jesus for whom she was weeping.

The encounter of Mary Magdalene with Jesus at the tomb is an extraordinary story. One aspect of the story from John's Gospel is worth noting: Mary Magdalene's weeping at the tomb. As mentioned earlier, this weeping is remembered four times in a few lines. Let us, therefore, reflect on the tears of this woman: Why did this woman weep at the tomb? The immediate answer is given by the same Gospel. Not only was she crying because her Lord was dead, but because she feared that even his tomb had been desecrated: "They have taken away my Lord, and I do not know where they have laid him" (John 20:13). But, beyond this first immediate reaction to a supposed fact, there is a deeper meaning to this woman who kept weeping despite the fact that she started to see in front of her the signs of the resurrection, that is, the empty tomb and the two angels instead of Jesus. Ultimately, the true answer to the question, "Woman, why are you weeping?" (John 20:15) should be worded as follows: "I am crying because I cannot understand the signs of the risen Lord; my eyes are so laden with tears that I cannot see signs of life; I cannot accept these comforting words."

For this woman who was almost shocked and deeply upset by Jesus' death, there was nothing but death around her; there could be nothing but death. Her mind seems almost fixated on the contemplation of Jesus' body and does not admit that there are other possibilities, that is, she does not accept that there is a way out from this circle of irreversible death.

Then, behind the question and the answer, behind the inconsolable weeping of this woman, we begin to glimpse something else, that is, first of all ourselves: we Christians, who also look for the Lord, and believe, and with our lips profess Jesus' resurrection, in which we deeply believe in our hearts, still find it hard to recognize the signs of the presence of the risen Christ within us. Or at times, we linger only to emphasize shortcomings, the signs of death and regrets. And, as this woman, who did not want to be consoled but persisted in her request of Jesus' body, we too find it hard to truly accept the transforming joy of the resurrection. Although weeping is painful, sometimes it is easier than accepting a great joy; easier than to open our hearts to an astonishing hope.

Mary Magdalene, then, who is the image of us Christians, becomes even more the image of humanity, and we might even say, the image of the city: many times in the Bible a city is represented as a woman (the daughter of Jerusalem weeping or rejoicing). This weeping woman represents the city that finds it hard to recognize the signs of the resurrection but clearly sees the signs of suffering around because they are many: disasters, kidnappings, violence, dishonesty, the arbitrary use of other people's money, the difficulty to accept peace proposals, moral disorder, the suppression of unborn life. We see all this and we linger—rightly so—to weep for all of this, but we also find it hard to see that this is but one side of the picture. We find it hard to see that this darker side is illuminated and transformed by the power of the Lord's resurrection. This power reaches every place and time, and we are called to prepare ourselves with a new mindset and a new culture to welcome it.

This first moment of disillusionment, of hesitation in recognizing the risen Christ is also found in the Acts of the Apostles. According to the account in Acts, we have the impression that the reality of the resurrection did not enter easily into the hearts of the apostles, as if it were a fact too great, too good, too sublime, too fraught with consequences, consequences difficult to imagine for the current way of understanding life.

The section of Acts dedicated to the resurrection is very dense and wants to describe briefly what characterized the short time in which Jesus, after his resurrection, appeared to the apostles and talked with them. That period of time is indicated by the reference to the forty days, perhaps a symbolic number designating a short time but still extensive enough to gradually realize and become aware of the fact that Jesus is truly risen and that this changes common perspectives and the way to look at life. This is one of the most dense pages of the Bible: in a few lines are comprised heaven and earth, the past of Jesus' life, the present of his stay with the apostles, the Church's future, the Father, the Son, and the Holy Spirit. And all this while the apostles were there, witnesses of these great events, who became signs and vessels of great revelations and on whom many promises were bestowed. And so, how did the apostles respond? Their reactions seem a little inadequate, almost clumsy: they appear somewhat confused.

Mary Magdalene's encounter with the risen Lord is a model of many other personal encounters with the risen Lord, with Jesus' life. Rereading it carefully, what strikes is the accuracy, the precision with which the gradual stages and subsequent moments that precede Mary Magdalene's recognition of the risen Lord are described in great detail. It is as if there are two parallel scenes, each marked by a series of actions that refer to each other; they are two actions that culminate in two questions that are essentially identical. The first, addressed by the two celestial figures—the two angels— and the second by Jesus himself. The questions are "Why are you weeping? Whom are you looking for?" (John 20:15). Mary's answer to this question is still confused, like that of someone who does not understand, who does not realize that those who ask the question actually already have the key to the mystery.

If we consider more in detail Mary's actions, which can be divided into two groups, we notice, analyzing the Greek text, that these actions are initially described in the past tense: "But Mary *stood weeping* outside the tomb. As she *wept*, she *bent* over to look into the tomb" (John 20:11, emphasis added). Then, at a certain point, the description goes from past to present tense: "And she sees two angels in white, sitting where the body of Jesus had been lying....They said to her, 'Woman, why are you weeping?' She said to them, 'They have taken away my Lord'" (John 20:12–13). The same happens in the next scene; it starts with the past tense: "She *turned* around and *saw* Jesus standing there, but she *did not know* that it was Jesus" (John 20:14, emphasis added) and then it switches to the present tense: "Jesus says, '...Whom are you looking for?'...She said to him, 'Sir, if you have carried him away, tell me where you have laid him....' Jesus said to her, 'Mary!'" (John 20:15–16).

We can observe in these two parallel scenes the description of a gradual and increasingly compelling realization until the final recognition expressed in the word "'Rabbouni!' (which means Teacher)" (John 20:16). A gradual, increasing realization that Jesus is alive, that Jesus is there, that Jesus is risen.

From this passage, therefore, we get the message that the encounter of humanity (because Mary here represents humanity; Mary Magdalene represents each one of us celebrating Easter) with the Divine, that is, the encounter of Mary Magdalene with the Divine is a slow and gradual encounter that requires subsequent stages, overcomings, separations (leaving behind one's conditioning and mental limits), and conversions. Mary Magdalene at the beginning is still closed within her own limits, in the narrow horizon of her questions, but as she is gradually invited by the unfolding events to leave behind what holds her back, she opens up to the recognition that Jesus was already there, alive in front of her. Therefore, leaving behind one's conditioning and mental limits, at a certain point, humanity faces Jesus, who is Truth and Life, who reveals himself with an effusive and astonishing immediacy that fills the human heart with enthusiasm and warmth that reverberates even in the body of those who share the joy of the Spirit.

Something similar to what is described regarding Mary Magdalene, which is actually the path of each one of us and of every man and woman, occurred to St. Augustine as well. The progressive knowledge that Augustine acquires of the risen Jesus allows scholars to speak in the plural of "St. Augustine's conversions"; thus, not only one conversion, but several, intending with that the various moments of his long journey from confusion to the spirit of faith.

The event of his baptism in 387 is the arrival point for St. Augustine after a long journey in which we can discern some milestones: the discovery of reason, the discovery of interiority, the discovery of grace, and the discovery of the Church. Augustine was a restless young man; he was very eager to learn more and more but did not think that the practices and rituals of the Church were good enough for him. When he was a young student, and then a young scholar, it seemed to him that even the stories of the Bible were for coarse and uneducated people, even though he continued to have great respect for his mother, Monica, who was a fervent Christian. He, however, believed that, being an intellectual, there was something better in store: gradually he shifted toward a strict form of rationalism, and then from rationalism to skepticism. While, with regard to a certain religious feeling, he was satisfied with ideological notions that allowed him, among other things, to think that one could have a Church without Christ and a morality without precepts. From this state of mental and theoretical confusion, the return to clarity was difficult and marked by progressive conversions.

Augustine's situation was similar to that of Mary Magdalene in John's Gospel: Mary Magdalene had the Lord next to her, but she still could not see him; Augustine, in his *Confessions*, says of himself something like, "You were within me, O Lord, and I outside. And it was there that I searched for you, where you were not. You were with me, but I was not with you." From here, from this recognition of confusion and unresolved, unsatisfied desire, began his arduous journey of conversion that mainly went from systematic doubt to the recognition that there are still some certainties, in this case the rediscovery of reason, and then, from a materialistic vision of life to a perception of the existence of a spiritual world and the discovery of interiority. Until this point, his journey back was still purely theoretical and accomplished with the help of the great pagan authors like Cicero and Plotinus, but at some point, he decided to move from a pure naturalism, from relying only on his own strength, to trust in grace and, finally, to the choice of a life totally dedicated to the search of truth within the real Church. Augustine found peace only when he fully accepted the doctrine of the Church.

Therefore, his progressive stages, corresponding in some way to the different stages of Mary Magdalene's recognition of Jesus, are in turn the discovery of reason, the discovery of interiority, the discovery of grace, and the discovery of the Church, which he rediscovered in the real Church of Milan and its bishop Ambrose. It is at this point that the very face of Christ was revealed to him again in all its glory.

In conclusion, regarding everything that as Christians we experience on Easter night, it is valid what Jesus said to Peter when he washed his feet: "You do not know now what I am doing, but later you will understand" (John 13:7). Only in part do we understand the things we do in the celebration of the holy night; we penetrate them in faith and anticipate them in hope; because if the events of Christ are already definite in him, as his resurrection, our participation is not. Therefore, what we live is all aimed toward that eternal wonder that will be for us also the revelation of the glory of Christ and his resurrection.

Therefore, it is good that we ask ourselves these questions: What has all this to do with the way we celebrate Easter? These eternal truths that reach the existence of every man and woman, what do they say to us today? Certainly, if we only look around, we can see that injustice, death, and loneliness still hold a tight grip on humanity, like a tragic and cursed noose. We cannot hide the fact that, even on Easter Sunday, in many countries of the world, there are threats and dramatic situations of conflict, death, injustice, and loneliness.

So what does the Easter event tell us? It tells us that these things are not the last word, that we cannot resign ourselves to these realities, that there is something we can do about them, and that God becomes our ally in this fight against injustice, death, and loneliness. God becomes our companion, filling our lives and allowing us to move from injustice, death, and loneliness to the reality of justice, truth, hope, and companionship with God, thus, also to the companionship of men and women with one another in the hope of eternal life.

So what is the final word that we receive at Easter from the events of Jesus' death and resurrection? The last word is left to us and it is the word of faith. We are asked, Do you accept the meaning of these events for your life, for the existence of the world? Do you welcome the life of Jesus who offers the overcoming of injustice, death, and loneliness? Do you welcome him for yourself? Do you welcome him for others? Are you ready to enter into this mystery of life and truth?

Everyone we encounter has the right to see in us a deep joy and a firm and creative hope; those who meet us need to hear the announcement, given to us and experienced by us, that Jesus is risen, that he lives, and that he has inaugurated a new life for himself and for all humanity.

Our human freedom, always ready to plan and program the future, looking always forward and ready to forget the past, which is often full of regrets and remorse, means also loyalty to a life that is given to us, to a story that came before us, to a task that is assigned to us by One who is bigger than us. There is also, with our freedom, our faithfulness to a name that someone gave us, our baptismal name; the faithfulness to the brothers and sisters entrusted to us; faithfulness, and trust, in a Father who has come toward us, who revealed himself in our history, declaring his love through Jesus, and who accepted his death to destroy our death.

Then, with a movement full of joy and confidence, our freedom of men and women adheres with faith to these gestures in which God is revealed, the gestures that are announced at every Easter Vigil in the long journey of our memory, and in this adherence, it finds its roots and the strength to walk toward the future with hope. Further, in this adherence of faith renewed in the Father who loves and is close to us, we find next to us the risen One, the living One who reunites in our lives past and future, filling our present with a dimension of eternity capable of embracing the things, people, situations, feelings, the suffering of the past and project it all, with love and faithfulness, toward a greater future, a confident future in which the risen One will always be at our side.

Jesus himself, risen and alive in the holy night of Easter, offers us a way to adhere to him: in the mysterious gestures of baptism and Eucharist. In baptism, catechumens are introduced into the living body of Christ and, through him, in the glorious past of the Church and the history of Israel. Through the Eucharist, we receive the body and blood of Christ; we adhere to Jesus who gave himself for us at the Last Supper, who gave us on the cross Mary as Mother, who in the Eucharist was nourishment for St. Peter, St. Paul, St. Ambrose, St. Charles, and all those who have gone before us in faith.

6. THE RISEN CHRIST IS WITH US

The paschal mystery is not a successive series of disparate events: Jesus is condemned; he goes through his passion; he dies on the cross; he is placed in the tomb; he rises after three days. These events should not be seen as separate or different from each other. What we should grasp instead in the paschal mystery is the fundamental unity in which Jesus' death and resurrection are part of a single mystery of salvation: the mystery of salvation in which humanity lives in Christ its passage from darkness to light, from solitude to communion, from despair to hope, from oppression to freedom, from death to life. It is this passage that is at the center of the prayer of praise that marks the beginning of the climax of the Easter Mass, that is, the beginning of the great Eucharistic Prayer. This is the Preface of Easter (it "introduces" the great Eucharistic Prayer), of the Easter Mass according to the Ambrosian rite, which reveals the effects of the Easter mystery in us, our human history, our personal and social lives.

Looking more closely at this prayer of thanksgiving, we can notice that it consists of four parts: it expresses a fundamental truth, which in turn is seen in the context of the history of salvation, then in the present, and finally, is sung in its wonderful effects. The fundamental assertion of this Easter prayer is ultimately, "Your Son Jesus Christ, though one with you in glory (*cum Deus esset maiestatis*), went to his death for our salvation."

Already here is all the sense of the paschal mystery: there is the mystery of the passionate involvement of God, eternal and invisible, with us, the inhabitants of this lonely planet and destined to die for our own sin. God wants to free us, and Christ Jesus offered himself for our salvation. The paschal mystery is therefore the mystery of the liberation of humanity, a mystery that affects us all, a gift that God gives to each one now, wherever we are on earth. This mystery of the liberation of humanity is rooted in the love of Jesus, Son of God, for every man and woman, a love that is beyond every human expectation, and which a contemporary religious poet defines as "almost an incurable disease of God for mankind. Only his mother understood it; his disease was his love for mankind, his disease was the love of the Father. That we do not love each other: that is his disease." This love of Jesus, which can almost be considered a disease of Christ for us, led him to bring to us the gift of liberation.

This gift had been prepared for a long time, and in the second part, the Preface recalls some great ancient prophecies of this gift: the sacrifice of Abraham's son, the Passover lamb, the foretold by Isaiah.

The third part of the Preface proclaims the fulfillment of the desire of human history in the Christian Easter. The prophet says this is the true Passover; that is, all the longing of history, both Jewish and universal, finds in it its fullness. What we are celebrating, as stated in the Preface, is the feast above all feasts; namely, that all human's ability to be glad and rejoice stems from this root; only starting from this solemnity can humanity live with confidence and rejoice: *solemnitatum omnium onoranda solemnitas* (the feast to be honored above all feasts), as written in the Preface.

The Preface ends with the singing of the following: "Now the prince of darkness (everything in life that makes us bitter and cynical) is vanquished; and we, drawn out from the depths of our fall (and the greatest sin is not believing that God loves us enough to give us his life), rejoice as we enter with the risen Savior in the Kingdom of Heaven." Christ is risen and we are partakers of his never-ending life. Only in this way can our human thoughts and plans take on a dimension and assurance that is given to them through the possibility of becoming part in the eternity of life that belongs to God, which is given to us in the risen Christ. Deliverance from death is the liberation that affects everything else and opens the way to every fruitful and lasting project of hope in humanity and its history.

Anyone who believes at least a little, who has at least a grain of faith, knows that one's vision of life actually leaves room for eternal life, for a life that never ends in the grace of Christ's redemption. This openness toward eternal life, even if only a tiny glimmer, determines a way of living and thinking that is illuminated by the light of Easter.

The passage from John's Gospel, which is read on Easter Sunday, ends with these words: "Mary Magdalene went and announced to the disciples, 'I have seen the Lord'" (John 20:18). In Mary Magdalene is proclaimed the cry of humanity facing Jesus' resurrection. "I have seen the Lord," "The Lord has risen indeed" (Luke 24:34), the Lord lives, "for he has been raised, as he said" (Matt 28:6): this simple statement, full of unfathomable depth, gradually reveals the richness of its meanings. First, it reveals something about the mystery of God. In fact, the ancient proclamation of the risen One was made with God in mind, as something about the mystery of God himself: God raised Jesus of Nazareth from the dead.

To the ancient blessings that came from the heart of the Jewish people, who deeply felt the mystery of God proclaiming "Blessed be God who made heaven and earth"; "Blessed be God who brought Israel out of Egypt"; "Blessed be God who drew his children out from the prison of death," we can now add these final and ultimate ones: "Blessed be God who saved Jesus from an apparently cursed death"; "Blessed be God who justified Jesus"; "Blessed be God who justified Jesus' life and death"; "Blessed be God who justified Jesus' proclamation of the Kingdom of Heaven, the beatitudes, and love of the poor"; "Blessed be God who has given assurance to humanity that Jesus of Nazareth's teachings—be merciful to sinners; denounce the danger of wealth and power; take the narrow way; proclaim the commandment of love—belong to God's truth." God the Father, by raising Jesus of Nazareth from the dead, has validated Jesus' life and death as the true way, as what pleases God, as what corresponds to God's plan. Therefore, this is God's will; God is revealed in the manner in which Jesus lived; this is who God is. Jesus' resurrection attests to this way of being of God, the God of the Gospel, of brotherhood, of the poor, of forgiveness, of love; the God of mercy, the God who does not want war but peace, the God of humility and meekness.

But there is even more. Through the proclamation of the risen Christ, we profess, together with the early Christians, that God is the one who knows how to be close to us in our suffering, disease, failure, misfortune, and death. God does not leave us alone and does not abandon us to death if we trust in God. Jesus cried out on the cross, "My God, my God, why have you forsaken me?" (Matt 27:46), but his resurrection showed that, though apparently abandoned by the Father who did not miraculously intervene to save him, Jesus is actually loved, justified, and welcomed by God.

Although God did not perform any miracles to save Jesus from death, God is always with Jesus, on his side, and validating him. Therefore, it is not through amazingly powerful miracles, but in being with each one of us in our trials, in keeping us company even in the deep recesses of our loneliness, in being close in our distress with the hope of eternal life that God reveals to be the "God with us," the God and Father of our Lord Jesus. God is everywhere someone suffers like Jesus, wherever someone dies like Jesus, wherever someone lives and suffers for love, for truth, for justice, for the poor; God is there to lessen the suffering of the world: this is the God of Jesus who is proclaimed by Jesus' resurrection.

Therefore, the Lord gives us a new and broader understanding of his mystery: God is not only the generative power that is revealed in the Creation of the world, but he is also the God who is revealed in the most tragic events of humanity, the God of Jesus' passion, agony, and death.

If then God is with Jesus to the point of death as shown in raising him from the dead, then we can understand the early Christians who realized how Jesus is with God in a very special way: Jesus is the Son whom the Father loved in death and beyond death; Jesus is the glorified Son; Jesus is the Son whose human nature the Father glorifies with that glory that had always been the Father's. If Jesus is the Son, if Jesus of Nazareth is with God, then we are with God, in Jesus. We are in God, and God is in us. The mystery of the covenant, of the unity of humanity with God, of our being one with the One who embraces everything, from which everything originates, of being one with the infinite mystery that is God: this is what is revealed to us in Jesus' Passover.

If Jesus, as Son, is in God and through his death, his own physical body has been glorified, even us, who believe in Jesus, are in God and our physical body carries within it the seed of the glory and fullness of being with God forever. We are God's eternal allies; God is ours because God possesses and is in us and with us in every instant of our existence.

God is in Jesus and is in each one of us just and precisely when we, like Jesus, humble ourselves; when we get closer to the least among us; when we become

118   Disciples of the Risen Christ

poor among the poor; when we imitate Jesus' lowering himself; when we imitate his ability of renouncing his privileges and demonstrations of power in order to be with the poor and the powerless. Jesus is with us and with all men and women of this world who follow consciously (and sometimes even without knowing it), this ministry of charity, of love, of service to the poor that is Jesus' way of life. Jesus is, thus, with us in all the complex and convoluted events of our human existence and in those of poor countries; he is with us in the most painful sufferings in so many parts of the world; in all the suffering, all the sorrows that lurk in the folds of our existence: diseases, failures, loneliness, divisions, anguish. Nothing is alien to Jesus' presence when, like him and with him, we rely on the will of the Father and live with love our daily existence.

Jesus is here, among us, not only as the horizon of our being Church, but as the living center of our being Church. Jesus is in us, not through the amazing power of miracles, which he used only in a very limited and modest way, but Jesus is in us with the continued, invisible, and mysterious presence of God's own mystery, of that light and almost imperceptible aura that is God's mystery, which, however, those who are born of God well understand in all the forms of expression of the presence of the risen Christ. Jesus is present in his Word proclaimed in the Scriptures and in the voice of the Church. Therefore, when we listen to his Word, we are in real communion with the risen Christ and our heart trembles with joy because it feels this intimate union, this inseparable relationship that has been established between us and the risen Christ, and that the proclaimed Word of God continually stimulates as a powerful electric current that activates the feelings in our hearts. Jesus is in us every time we receive the sacraments, whenever we perform the sacramental gestures and utter the sacramental words, in which Jesus, risen and alive, is felt.

Jesus is in the heart of every man and woman who believes and hopes; Jesus is in the heart of humanity that belongs to him, and of his Church. Jesus is there where he is celebrated, where he is loved. The risen Christ is there where two or three are gathered in his name. Jesus is in the least among us, in the sick, the imprisoned, the marginalized, the lonely foreigner without means. Jesus is in those who are abandoned and derelict. Jesus is with the poorest people in the world. Jesus is in the dark folds of those families where there is suffering, rejection, inability to bear one another, and pain. Jesus enters where there is suffering of all types and can vivify and transform it with the power of his Holy Spirit.

In his resurrection, Jesus has revealed the secret of his cross, the secret of his death out of love, the secret of his suffering offered to God. God is with us, the Father will resurrect us with Jesus; God the Father promises us eternal life and, as of now, the fullness of life in the Holy Spirit and the gift of the risen Son.

At any time, Jesus' Passover is in us and among us as an inexhaustible source of life and as a presence that we can already experience in the communion of the Easter Vigil, in intense prayer, in the impulses of the heart, in the deep and incomprehensible joy that, at times, envelops us. This Passover is in us and with us when we hear the Word of God, when we eat and we are nourished by his body and his blood, when we receive the baptismal waters.

The risen Christ is in us, in the face of every brother and sister who is near; he is in the sacraments and in the Church. Therefore, he is in human history: he is in us and with us for sharing with us an absolutely new life; a sharing that preserves and exceeds the state of this human existence, giving it dimensions of eternity, sublimating it in fullness, in glory, in spirituality, pushing us toward a moral, spiritual, and social renewal of this earthly life; a life that we then live with joy and fullness, with an eye to our eternal destiny. What matters is the faith in Easter, this faith that is the foundation of hope, a source of joy and inner peace.

Of course, daily life should be lived today as yesterday; it should be lived and considered realistically, facing its difficulties, but without losing sight of its unshakable principle: we are certain that as a whole and in the unfolding of the great and small events of each day the risen Christ is with us, he has won for us the powers of evil, of sin, of banality, frustration, boredom, and death. For him and with him, we can overcome evil with good, drawing from the greatest evil an even greater good. This is the strength and novelty of Easter that we live especially on Easter Sunday.

Thus, we can also encounter and "touch" the risen Christ in our everyday life, not in extraordinary facts or events, because this unique, extraordinary, and definitive event that encompasses all others, that is, Jesus' resurrection, is present and alive in our midst.

We feel that this new world that Jesus has inaugurated was accomplished for us and is also in our midst. We feel, therefore, that Jesus' Passover is a true re-creation, a new creation of humanity. For this reason, in the readings of the Easter Vigil, the Church makes us reflect on some of God's amazing deeds from the very beginning: the world's creation, the temptation of Abraham, the exodus from Egypt, the great prophecies. All these events tell us that everything finds its climax in Jesus' resurrection, that it is all here, and here for us. We are the new creation freed from the darkness of evil and sin; we are involved in the new birth of humanity that begins with Jesus.

Our faith is not based simply on the discovery of the empty tomb, but on all Jesus' apparitions that are announced in the pages of the Gospel ("He is going ahead of you to Galilee; there you will see him," Mark 16:7), where Jesus rebuilds and heals all human relations: those of friendship and brotherly affection, of collaborative work and apostolate service, of bearing legal witness for others, and around the eucharistic table. Everything is re-created and all human relationships and all our ways of communicating are reinvented, as they are invested by the power of Jesus' life. So our relationships, on earth, already become the beginning of our future relationships in heaven. All our authentic relationships here on earth already touch the hem of the garment of the risen Christ and make us foresee and anticipate the perfect relationship of us all, among ourselves and with God, for eternity, in the heavenly Jerusalem. All this started with Jesus' resurrection. All this, therefore, is accomplished for us on the Easter Vigil. On that night we already touch eternity.

The First Epistle to the Corinthians is the earliest evidence, the earliest record we possess of the Christian faith in the risen One, and it dates back to the earliest years after Jesus' death. In this page, Paul says, "For I handed on to you as of first importance what I in turn had received" (15:3). Thus, in writing this letter in the first decades of the Christian era, Paul's account goes even further back to what he was told during his encounter in Damascus with the risen One, and even to what the apostles in Jerusalem, shortly after, communicated to him. We are thus in front of a formula that dates back to the earliest days of the Christian faith, the earliest one in the New Testament. Paul here proclaims that Christ died, was buried, was raised, appeared to Cephas, then to the Twelve, and then to many others (see 1 Cor 15:3–6).

In this passage, there are four verbs that are attributed to Christ: three are in that verbal mode in the original Greek, indicating a precise fact that occurred in the past (*he died, was buried, he appeared*); but the fourth verb (*was raised*) is in the Greek tense, indicating a past action that has its effect in the present. Therefore, Jesus is not only risen but lives today for us and for the entire world. Jesus' resurrection is nothing but the culminating moment of the fullness of God's life and love that is communicated to humanity in Christ Jesus; this fullness continues to grow through humanity's acceptance, along its path, of the grace of Christ, the risen One.

We can truly say then that the power of Jesus' resurrection has never been greater than today through the multitude of saints, confessors, martyrs, men and women of faith, the hundreds of millions, the billions throughout human history from Christ to the present who have welcomed his message, have been transformed by it, and now live the divine life of the risen Christ. This message, therefore, is alive for us, and in its unfolding, is at its all-time high; it is even stronger somehow, historically speaking, from the point of view of its effects than not two thousand years ago: it is here, alive and powerful, for us and in us.

Through baptism, Christ is in us, lives in us, walks with us, and asks us to become part with him of the history of the world, transforming it, giving up all selfishness, opening ourselves to everyone; opening ourselves to love, forgiveness, patience, humility, tolerance, generosity, kindness, and many other things that we can summarize in one word: Jesus calls us to holiness.

In a homily of the Easter Vigil, Cardinal Schuster, Archbishop of Milan, once described the feast that celebrates this most significant and present event as follows: "In the Gospel there is a fact that I find very important: the first Christian Easter took place at a tomb, where an angel spoke of resurrection. The angel wants us to take part in Christ's feast because it truly is the feast of all of us, the living and the dead. Today, Jesus opens the way to eternal life, inaugurating a path of truth, of holiness, and vital energy." Then he added, "Jesus' Passover would not be complete if it didn't join our Passover. He wants to arise in us to cure our hidden sores and wounds; and it must be a celebration in the whole world, so that all men and women may know that they have been saved and forgiven by the blood of Jesus, the Crucified and Risen One."

7. LIVING AS RESURRECTED

Thus, a new condition and a new horizon emerge in the world in which we are now called to live. No doubt, in this horizon there is still fatigue and daily suffering. Sin surrounds us, but we already know that if we are united with the risen Christ, it cannot do us any harm, it can no longer poison our lives or kill us.

We must make this great announcement to others, telling them that they too are and can become children of God; that they can live as children of God, take part in Jesus' resurrection, and feel that God is always with them in everyday life.

What emerges is the missionary proclamation of the Church, the responsibility to go out and announce the good news that we entrust in particular to our brothers and sisters who receive the sacraments of Christian initiation on the Easter Vigil, and thus, are sent as children of God to go and announce to everyone that they can become children of God, live as children of God, enter in Jesus' resurrection. Being raised in baptism means in fact to live as newly risen ones, repeating the message, propagating the flame that comes to us through the gift of the Holy Spirit in the sacrament of confirmation.

Easter then becomes an invitation to a serious and responsible commitment of faith for all of us, an invitation to testify in our flesh and in our life the wonderful deeds of Jesus of Nazareth, confident that the risen One gives us the opportunity to live them. Easter becomes an invitation to walk from death to life every day to show that love is stronger than selfishness, hope is stronger than every disappointment, light is stronger than darkness, the Holy Spirit is above the law.

We may ask ourselves at this point what would happen to us if we let this light enter into our lives not only from a crack, but in full; by opening doors and windows to the risen Christ, just as we do to welcome the spring sunshine; as a different way of seeing our work, our family relationships, often so tense and cold, our real or feared diseases, the illnesses and sufferings of our loved ones, the painful separations that mark our lives, or that will mark us inevitably. All these realities acquire a different meaning, a different dimension when seen in the light of Easter: everything is likely to be redeemed by hope.

Christ gives us life, hope, a mission, and a future, with the certainty, therefore, that none of our personal or social situations, difficult as they may be, are really irredeemable, and that we must do our part, with Christ who is our life, to heal with our love tense or stressful situations in our midst.

But in order for Jesus' resurrection to truly be the bliss of our being, we must come out from the tomb in our heart and believe that he is here with us now, walking with us; that he is the source of our life; and that he will be it until the last day of this world. The message of

Easter is therefore the message of the infinite love of God for man. The whole history of the world is founded on one single miracle: God's mercy that freely redeems us to pour forth in us the revelation of who God is, that is, infinite love.

The paschal mystery is the fundamental act of God for humankind, and now we can experience it, again and again, in every Eucharist so as to have the strength to be faithful to our condition as children of God in order to experience the effects of Christ's resurrection. Therefore, Christ's resurrection is neither a dream nor utopia; it is the realism of the Gospel on which we base our notions of life, history, ethics, and civilization. For this reason, even in our often sad and contradictory reality, where words like *peace*, *freedom*, *hope* often find a land too dry in which to grow, we shout the good news of the resurrection; with our life and our words, we must proclaim to the world that Jesus has risen for all. It is he who gives us the strength to face our century's difficult and disturbing questions; it is he who gives us the ability to understand our society and act in it and upon it in line with the principles of life.

Easter calls us to live as risen ones in the certainty that the future is full of hope because it is the future of the perfect and total redemption of humankind, of history, and of the universe; Easter calls us to live as Jesus lived, participating in his trials and his cross to let the power of his resurrection work in us.

The angels, who sang on Christmas night, who served Jesus in the desert, and who comforted him in his agony, approach the tomb, roll the stone, and say to the women gathered at the sepulcher, "Do not be alarmed; you are looking for Jesus of Nazareth, who was crucified. He has been raised; he is not here" (Mark 16:6). "Do not be afraid!" is the invitation that the risen One today continues to address to all of us, to save us, forgive us, justify us, reconcile us, and give us new life.

It is therefore necessary that we pray to the Lord with these words: may in faith, hope, and charity we become able to proclaim to the world that Christ is risen and dies no more, and that he rose again to give new and eternal life to all men and women on earth.

|||

Pentecost: The Fulfillment of the Easter Mystery

1. THE SPIRIT OF RENEWAL

The first part of the second chapter of the Acts of the Apostles describes the event of Pentecost, which appears as an enigmatic and mysterious event that raises a question about its meaning. This question is answered by Peter's speech in which he explains its significance in the light of Jesus' resurrection and ascension. Peter's speech is followed by another event, the conversion of three thousand people, after which there is a community: the newly formed early Church listening to the Word, in prayer, around the eucharistic table. All these events reveal something of the mystery of the Holy Spirit.

To understand the second chapter of the Acts of the Apostles better, it is useful to read it together with chapter 20 of John's Gospel. The intrinsic link between these two readings was expressed by John Paul II in his encyclical on the Holy Spirit titled *Dominum et Vivificantem*. Speaking of the account of Pentecost in the Acts of the Apostles, John Paul II said, "This event constitutes the definitive manifestation of what had already been accomplished in the same Upper Room on Easter Sunday. The Risen Christ came and 'brought' to the Apostles the Holy Spirit. He gave him to them, saying 'Receive the Holy Spirit'" (John 20:22). He then added, "What had then taken place inside the Upper Room, 'the doors being shut,' later, on the day of Pentecost is manifested also outside, in public. The doors of the Upper Room are opened and the Apostles go to the inhabitants and the pilgrims who had gathered in Jerusalem on the occasion of the feast, in order to bear witness to Christ in the power of the Holy Spirit."

Therefore, we can say that the event of Pentecost, described in the Acts of the Apostles on the fiftieth day after Easter, is the external, ecclesial, public manifestation of that event experienced in the intimacy of the Last Supper by the apostles with the resurrected Jesus who had brought them the Holy Spirit.

Fifty days after Easter Sunday, we celebrate and relive the mystery of Pentecost, the fulfillment of the Easter mystery. We celebrate the fire of Jesus' love that his Spirit spread to the Church so it can reach the entire world, a fire that will never end. Pentecost continues in each eucharistic assembly. It is the Spirit who transforms the bread and wine into Jesus' broken body and shed blood; it is the invocation of the Spirit that becomes the cry of the Church, the mystery of faith, and allows us to announce in every Eucharist the death of our Lord and proclaim his resurrection; it is the Spirit that creates the Christian community not as a simple gathering of good and religious people, but as the mystical body of Christ, the body gathered in the love of the Trinity.

What began with the power of the Spirit today is regenerated and renewed not through words, programs, conferences, or other human initiatives, but by reviving its strength in the Holy Spirit. The Holy Spirit is the One who continually renews the Church; the Holy Spirit renews our lives, so often weary, weak, troubled, fearful, and withdrawn into themselves. We are not renewed through human reasoning, but through this power of the Spirit given to us in the sacraments, in the Eucharist, in prayer. This is power of the Spirit that the Lord continually pours upon us—if we open our arms and hearts. In the Gospel passage, we read about the irruption of the Spirit and the beginning of the gift of tongues. In his account, the evangelist Luke is inspired by the liturgical significance that the Jewish feast of Pentecost had assumed at the time of Jesus. This ancient feast, celebrated fifty days after Passover, which originally was the harvest festival, subsequently became the feast of the renewal of the covenant and thus recalled the gift of the law at Mount Sinai. At Pentecost, the rush of the wind and the fire recall the appearance of God, the theophany at Mount Sinai. The rushing wind is a sign of God's irruption in the world, of God who takes hold of the human creature as he took hold of Jesus, of God who takes hold of every believer. The rushing wind is thus the sign of the new humanity in the Spirit.

With Pentecost begins the last days of the new and eternal covenant, the time of the Church generated and animated by the Spirit. Through this Spirit in us, the sacraments acquire validity and strength, and the body of the Church grows in the grace of holiness. It is this Spirit that transforms us inwardly, making us act in the spirit of the Beatitudes. It is this Spirit that purifies us by creating in us a new sensibility, a new taste for the spiritual things of God.

When Jesus says, "Receive the Holy Spirit" (John 20:22), he is speaking of the Spirit of God, the source of creation, the origin of a new human life, the One who frees humankind from sin. It is the Spirit of God that infuses in each one of us an ever-new dimension of joy, peace, truth, freedom, and communion. By transforming us into new creatures, the Spirit allows us to follow in Jesus' footsteps toward the Father. It is this journey, this exodus, in communion with the whole Church that those who receive the sacrament of confirmation undertake: a choice of life consecrated by the Holy Spirit to live according to the spirit of the Beatitudes.

The presence of the Spirit is the condition without which we cannot achieve God's plan of salvation.

2. THE CELEBRATION OF THE BIRTH OF THE CHURCH

The episode of the gift of the Holy Spirit by Jesus is told in two moments of the Scriptures: in Luke's Gospel and in the Acts of the Apostles.

Looking first at Luke's Gospel, it is interesting to note the relationship between the scene described in the Gospel on Easter Sunday and the one described by Luke fifty days after Easter—*Pentecost* means "fifty"—to try to understand for what purpose Luke decided to put the Pentecost narrative at the beginning of his account of the early Church. Luke wanted his readers to understand that after Jesus' resurrection, the most important and determining fact in the life of the Church is the outpouring of the Holy Spirit on the believers.

In short, these are the testimonies of the early Church: we felt less fear and a growing enthusiasm; we felt an increasing clarity on what we had to do; we saw the divisions of languages, races, cultures disappear in front of our eyes before the only Gospel. From all this, we understood that a great gift was given to us, a divine gift: God was drawing close to each of us, giving us an energy of love and a regenerating power of our lives, that is, resurrection from death. We understood that this force was the Holy Spirit.

Luke tries to convey all these things in a very short, almost terse, page. He mentions all this in connection with the early Church so we can understand that this is the Church, this is the life of the Church, this is the history of the Church: a history, a life aroused, animated, promoted, supported by the outpouring of the Holy Spirit. This is what Luke wants to express with this first account of Pentecost: what the Church is. Not only what it was, but what it is every day under the transforming and renewing action of the Spirit of Christ.

While the Gospel passage speaks of the new life that comes from the forgiveness of sins, the passage from Acts recounts the gift of the Spirit for the Church first by using the symbol of the rushing wind that fills the entire house, and then by speaking of the languages that in unison proclaim the glory of God and Jesus' wonderful deeds.

Therefore, we can see in the story of Acts how the nucleus of the first community (120 disciples gathered together with the eleven apostles and Mary) was enriched by a generative and dynamic principle, a principle that will set in motion the whole process of expansion and implementation of the Church in the world: this generative and dynamic principle is the gift of the Holy Spirit.

The second chapter of the Acts of the Apostles, whose first part we read during the liturgy of Pentecost, is structured according to three major realities: the Spirit, the word, and life. First, the Spirit: the first lines of the reading describe the coming of the Spirit as a fulfillment of Jesus' promise through the signs of the wind and of the tongues of fire. From the Spirit we move to the word: at first it is a word proclaimed in a generic way as praise of God (the apostles announce God's mighty works in different languages), then it becomes more specific in the rest of Acts 2 with Peter's first major speech. Therefore, as we witness the descent of the Spirit and listen to the proclamation of the word, we witness the birth of the first Christian community: people are amazed at what they see and hear, they are intrigued and ready to listen to Peter, and after listening to him, they ask, "What should we do?" (Acts 2:37). Thus, the Spirit and the word give life to the primitive Christian community, sanctified by baptism and formed through hearing the apostles' word, through prayer, through communal life, through the breaking of the bread.

This is precisely what the different images in this episode signify: the rushing wind that fills the house, the tongues of fire, the single language understood by many. This is the founding event of the Church, presented here for the first time in its fullness of the Spirit. The Church is not born of power or human decision, but from the gift of the Holy Spirit.

This is the entire event that we celebrate on the feast of Pentecost: the irruption of the Spirit, of the word, and the life that creates and shapes the Church. This Church of ours, to which we are proud to belong, this Church that was born from Jesus' death and resurrection is realized through the gift of the Spirit, the power of the word, and the response of life.

At Pentecost, we celebrate the very birth of the Church, as stated by the same words of the Second Vatican Council: "When the work which the Father gave the Son to do on earth was accomplished, the Holy Spirit was sent on the day of Pentecost in order that He might continually sanctify the Church, and thus, all those who believe would have access through Christ in one Spirit to the Father" (*Lumen Gentium* 4).

The feast of Pentecost reminds us that the Church was born charismatic, spiritual, pneumatic, that is, from a divine bestowal of the Spirit and not from a human project off the drawing board. After Jesus' resurrection, the apostles did not consult with one another saying, "How are we going to fulfill the mandate of the Lord? How are we going to reach all people? How are we going to fulfill Jesus' ministry in this problematic society?" These were, after all, legitimate questions. Perhaps they even asked these questions, but the Lord exhorted them not to make plans, but to sit and wait for the Spirit. This is what they did in Jerusalem, and it will be the Spirit that guides them and suggests how and where to start, what to say, and what to do. It will be the Spirit that will give them enthusiasm, momentum, agility, intuition. This is how the Church was born, and it is the Spirit that gives life to the Church today. It is with this confidence that every year we celebrate the feast of Pentecost.

The tongues of fire, by which the Spirit fills each of us, seal this unique and personal relationship of each one of us with the Trinity; it is a sign of God who enters into each one of us as an enlightening and consuming fire that then becomes Word in the Church.

From this wind and fire emerges the gift of tongues. As the multiplicity of languages of the tower of Babel revealed the fracture and the confusion of humanity, now the multiplicity of languages, which communicate and are understood, marks the beginning of the universality of the Church, the one body of Christ announcing in one language the greatness of God. Pentecost is not therefore, in itself, simply the feast of the Holy Spirit as we commonly believe (the feast of the Holy Spirit is celebrated every Sunday, in every liturgy, in every sacrament). Rather, at Pentecost we celebrate the historical celebration of the beginning of the Church in the power of the Spirit.

In fact, every liturgical celebration in the Church is the celebration of an event, of a historical fact: first of all, the events and historical facts about Jesus, such as his birth, his life, his passion, his death, and his resurrection; and then, in connection with Jesus, also the events concerning Mary, Jesus' Mother, from her immaculate conception to her assumption. All our feasts celebrate the incarnate Word or something that pertains to it. What event about Jesus is commemorated on the day of Pentecost? It is his presence in the Church through the Holy Spirit. Thus, it is the feast of Jesus' Church that lives in Jesus' Spirit. It is the feast of all of us who, in the sacraments, starting with baptism, have become Church. We have become and continue to be one with Jesus through the gift of his Spirit.

3. PROMISE AND TESTIMONY

The fact of the outpouring of the gift of the Holy Spirit upon the believers did not happen only once. The testimony of the New Testament speaks of numerous events of the outpouring of the Holy Spirit. The same account in Acts 4 speaks of an outpouring on the disciples, which occurred as they prayed in fear because of the start of the persecutions: "The place in which they were gathered together was shaken; and they were all filled with the Holy Spirit" (4:31). The evangelist Luke recounts, in chapter 8, the outpouring of the Holy Spirit upon the inhabitants of Samaria; chapter 10 narrates the outpouring of the Holy Spirit upon Cornelius, the Roman centurion, and all those of his house; and finally, chapter 19 describes the Holy Spirit descending on a dozen disciples who in Ephesus received baptism and the laying on of hands.

Therefore, there are many outpourings of the Holy Spirit, and Luke has collected from all of these accounts and evidences some fundamental beliefs and principles of the disciples that can be broadly summarized as follows: since Jesus died, we have not been alone. Not only has he risen and has manifested himself several times for his own; but not even since we have no longer seen him, not even after his resurrection, has he left us alone: a power from above has guided us in these difficult events of the journey of the first churches. We felt and feel inside of us a new vital energy, as an augmentation of forces, an enhancement of our soul, and we feel that it is the gift of God: like a hurricane, a beneficial wind that shakes us and penetrates us all; hence, we understand that the risen Christ realized his promise: "And I will ask the Father, and he will give you another Advocate, to be with you forever....I will not leave you orphaned" (John 14:16, 18). It is in the Acts of the Apostles that the fulfillment of Jesus' promise is described, what he had done to his disciples before ascending to heaven, saying: "I am sending upon you what my Father promised; so stay here in the city until you have been clothed with power from on high" (Luke 24:49). They are promised the "power from on high," and we can see that it is the same promise that was made to Mary at the annunciation: "The Holy Spirit will come upon you, and the power of the Most High will overshadow you" (Luke 1:35). We have heard and understood that the God of our Fathers realized his promise made by the prophets of late: "I will send my Spirit on everyone: the young, the old, those who are well off, those who are suffering. On all. The healthy and the sick." We understood, the early

Christians said, what had happened and what God did for our fathers in the desert, after the first Passover in Egypt, giving the law at Sinai. Thus, fifty days after Passover, God put the law of the Spirit in our hearts.

Today, we are not inferior in any way to the early Christians in terms of grace and gifts received. Indeed, the power of the ecclesial communion, the strength of all the saints, of all the witnesses of the faith, the intercession of Mary, the experiences of the Church over the centuries urge us to look to the task of evangelization with realism, and, no doubt, also with a sense of pain for all those who close their ears and hearts; but along with renewed confidence that the Holy Spirit is poured out, without measure, today by God to those who humbly ask for it.

Cardinal Giovanni Colombo said, in fact, in a homily on Pentecost of 1971, "Faced with the desolate landscape of decadence, the first grievance and the first accusation should be brought against us Christians, our conscience, and our behavior. Because the Holy Spirit has entrusted us with the mission to be witnesses of faith in Christ, who died and rose again."

We certainly do not want to be like some of those who, closing their doors and hearts, say: "Enough; I'm discouraged and don't care; things will always be the same anyway"; this is a sin against the Holy Spirit of God who, even today, as before, is ready to pour out his grace on those who open their hearts, in every part of the world, to God's merciful power.

John's Gospel tells us that after the resurrection, Jesus appeared to the apostles, stood among them, twice he gave his peace, showed the signs of the wounds of the crucifixion, and shared his mission with them: "As the Father has sent me, so I send you" (John 20:21).

Not for nothing, in his twelfth encyclical entitled *Ut Unum Sint*, which is clearly a Pentecostal encyclical, Pope John Paul II said, "The Church is not a reality closed in on herself. Rather, she is permanently open to missionary and ecumenical endeavour, for she is sent to the world to announce and witness, to make present and spread the mystery of communion which is essential to her, and to gather all people and all things into Christ, so as to be for all an 'inseparable sacrament of unity.'"

In this regard, it can be useful to reflect on a specific detail in the account of the descent of the Spirit in the Acts of the Apostles, that is, the list of people who are the witnesses of Pentecost. Exegetes have long sought to understand the why and the origin of this long list of seventeen names divided into several categories: there are three names of people (Parthians, Medes, Elamites); then, there are nine names of regions and countries (Mesopotamia, Judea and Cappadocia, Pontus, Asia, Phrygia, Pamphylia, Egypt, Libya near Cyrene); there are also names of general categories (visitors from Rome, Jews, and proselytes), and religious categories; and finally two names (Cretans and Arabs) that seem to indicate the people from the islands, such as Crete and those from the mainland.

It is almost a map of the missions of the early Church; as if from Jerusalem, or from another primitive community, like that of Antioch in Syria, they are contemplating the map of the territories to be evangelized. Certainly, this map goes back to the very beginning of Christianity because it is clearly all focused on eastern territories. In fact, great importance is given to the countries of the near East and very little, instead, to the western ones. The massive shift of Christianity to the West had not occurred yet. Therefore, it is a first attempt to draw the map of the missions and, above all, to indicate that from its very beginning, the Church embraces with love many people, many countries, many languages regardless of culture, race, and education. In short, it is a proclamation of the universality, from the very beginning, of the people of God.

The Spirit, therefore, opens our heart to the entire world. We find it hard to overcome the racial and ethnic barriers even in the streets of our cities. But the Holy Spirit works in a different way. It works by opening our hearts, making us realize that we are brothers and sisters, leading us in one another's arms by removing the obstacles that create divisions among us: this is the path of the Spirit, the path of humankind, of a reconciled humanity. We must commit ourselves to this path of the Church, to this journey that is directed by the power of the Holy Spirit.

We can summarize the Pentecostal message in one simple invitation: "You go into my vineyard too." These are the words recalled by John Paul II in his encyclical on the lay faithful (*Christifideles Laici*), according to which the call of the Lord Jesus, "You go into my vineyard too," never fails to resound throughout history, and is addressed to every man and woman in this world, even in our times. In the renewed outpouring of the Spirit of Pentecost that occurred with the Second Vatican Council, the Church has gained a deeper awareness of her missionary nature: "You go too," said Pope John Paul II. The call is not just for pastors, priests, religious men and women, but is extended to everyone: even laypeople are personally called by the Lord, from whom they receive a mission on behalf of the Church and the world: "The lay faithful ought to regard themselves as an active and responsible part of this venture, called as they are to proclaim and to live the gospel in service to the person and to society while respecting the totality of the values and needs of both," continued John Paul II. The entire Church, pastors and faithful, must feel stronger the responsibility to obey Christ's command: "Go into all the world and proclaim the good news to the whole creation" (Mark 16:15), renewing her missionary zeal. A great, challenging, and wonderful mission is entrusted to the Church: that of a new evangelization, of which the world today is in great need. The lay faithful must feel to be actively and responsibly involved in this mission, called as they are to proclaim and live the Gospel in service to the values and needs of humanity and society.

Be my witnesses; be my witnesses in these difficult times; be my witnesses, says the Lord on the day of Pentecost, especially to the young. As Pope John Paul II always stressed, "Young people are and ought to be encouraged to be active on behalf of the Church as *leading characters in evangelization and participants in the renewal of society*....The sensitivity of young people profoundly affects their perceiving of the values of justice, nonviolence and peace. Their hearts are disposed to fellowship, friendship and solidarity. They are greatly moved by causes that relate to the quality of life and the conservation of nature" (*Christifideles Laici*). Be my witnesses then you young ones.

If we ask, "Where, O Lord, do you want us to be your witnesses?" The Lord will answer: in this land, in this culture, in this society, in this region that God has given us as a gift of the covenant so that we can nurture it for our brothers and sisters, in justice and peace.